Reboarnd 1997

977

'c may be kept

)URTEEN D

ged for eac' ay th

THE TASTE OF OUR TIME

Collection planned and directed by

ALBERT SKIRA

BIOGRAPHICAL AND CRITICAL STUDY

BY

JACQUES LASSAIGNE

Translated by Stuart Gilbert

MATISSE

SKIRA

Title page:
Blue Nude, 1952. Cut and pasted paper.
Private Collection, Paris.

*

Distributed by Crown Publishers, Inc.
419 Park Avenue South, New York, N.Y. 10016

© 1959 by Editions d'Art Albert Skira, Geneva
Library of Congress Catalog Card Number: 59-12318
New edition 1972

CHRONOLOGICAL SURVEY

1869 December 31, Henri Emile Benoît Matisse born at Le Cateau-Cambrésis (Nord), in the house of his grandfather Emile Gérard in the Rue du Chêne-Arnaud (now renamed Rue de la République).
His father and mother, Emile and Anna Matisse (née Gérard), live at 24, Rue Fayard, Bohain-en-Vermandois; here Henri spends his childhood and early youth.
Attends the Lycée at Saint-Quentin, taking the classics course.

1887-1888 Studies law at the University of Paris. Obtains certificate qualifying him to practise as a lawyer.

1889 Clerk in the law office of Maître Duconseil at Saint-Quentin.

1890 When convalescing after an operation for appendicitis amuses himself copying the "chromo" landscapes on a box of paints given him by his mother. Attends drawing classes at the Ecole Quentin de La Tour, while continuing to work in the law office.

1891 His father having reluctantly consented to his going to Paris to study art, Matisse enrolls in the Académie Julian, where he is coached by Bouguereau and Ferrier for the entrance examination of the Ecole des Beaux-Arts.

1892 Meets Albert Marquet at the evening classes of the Ecole des Arts Décoratifs.

1895 His work catches the eye of Gustave Moreau, who invites Matisse to join the class in his studio, exempting him from the preliminary examination. His fellow students are Rouault, Desvallières, Piot, Simon-Bussy, Evenepoel, Baignères; then, a little later, Flandrin, Camoin, Manguin, Linaret.
In summer first trip to Brittany (Beuzec-Cap Sizun).
Settles into a studio at 19, Quai Saint-Michel, Paris, where his nextdoor neighbor is Emile Wéry.
Does a series of copies at the Louvre, along with his fellow students.

1895 Gauguin's second voyage to the South Seas.
Cézanne Exhibition at Vollard's.

1896 Matisse exhibits at the Salon de la Société Nationale des Beaux-Arts. His "Woman Reading" bought by the State and hung in the President's residence, the Château de Rambouillet. Summer: second trip to Brittany and Belle-Ile, where he meets J. P. Russell, American friend of Van Gogh and Monet.

1897 His "Dinner Table" shown at the Salon de la Nationale. Returns to Belle-Ile.
Meets Camille Pissarro.

1898 Marries Amélie Noémi Alexandrine Parayre. Honeymoon at London, where he looks at the Turners. Then a long stay in Corsica followed up by one in the neighborhood of Toulouse (his wife's hometown) and at Fenouillet.

1898 Death of Mallarmé and Gustave Moreau.
The "Nabis" exhibit at Durand-Ruel's.

1899 Exhibits for the last time at the Nationale. Leaves the École des Beaux-Arts where Cormon has replaced Gustave Moreau. With Marquet, paints from life in the Luxembourg gardens, at Arcueil, and from his window on the Quai Saint-Michel. Buys from Vollard Cézanne's "Three Bathers" (which he presented to the Musée du Petit-Palais in 1936).
Attends the Académie Carrière, Rue de Rennes, where he meets Derain, Biette and Puy, and studies sculpture in the evening classes of the free municipal school on the Rue Etienne-Marcel.

1900 Financial straits; works with Marquet for the decorator Jambon on the frieze of the Grand-Palais. Mme Matisse opens a milliner's shop on the Rue de Chateaudun.

1900 Derain meets Vlaminck at Chatou.
Picasso's first stay in Paris.
Centennial of French Art at the Paris World's Fair.

1901 Begins to exhibit at the Salon des Indépendants.
Goes to Switzerland to convalesce after an attack of bronchitis.

1901 Van Gogh Retrospective at Bernheim-Jeune's.

1902 Begins to exhibit at Berthe Weill's, Rue Victor-Massé.
Spends winter with his parents at Bohain.

1902 Lautrec Retrospective at the Indépendants.

1903 Exhibits two paintings at the newly founded Salon d'Automne, and thereafter exhibits there regularly.

1903 Death of Gauguin and Pissarro.

1904 June. First one-man show at Vollard's, catalogue prefaced by Roger Marx.
Summer at St Tropez with Signac and Cross.

1904 Exhibition of French Primitives at the Pavillon de Marsan, Paris.

1905 Exhibits major works at the Indépendants ("Luxe, calme et volupté"); also figures in the "central cage" of the Fauve gallery at the Salon d'Automne.
First purchases by the Steins, and support from Marcel Sembat.
Summer at Collioure where Derain comes to join him. Strikes up a friendship with Maillol, who takes him to visit Daniel de Monfreid, custodian of most of Gauguin's South Seas pictures.

1905 Seurat and Van Gogh Retrospectives at the Indépendants.
Manet Retrospective at the Salon d'Automne.
Foundation of "Die Brücke" at Dresden.

1906 The "Joy of Life" at the Indépendants.
Second one-man show at Galerie Druet.
After a brief trip to Biskra, spends the summer at Collioure.
First lithographs and woodcuts.

1906 Gauguin Retrospective at the Salon d'Automne.
Death of Cézanne.

1907 Journey to Italy.
"Le Luxe" at the Salon d'Automne.

1907 Picasso's "Demoiselles d'Avignon." Marquet exhibition at Druet's. Cézanne Retrospective at the Salon d'Automne and the Bernheim-Jeune Gallery.

1908 At the suggestion of Sarah Stein and Hans Purrmann, Matisse starts a painting class in a studio he had rented for painting "Joy of Life." He moves the school, greatly increased in numbers, to the disused Couvent du Sacré Cœur, 33 Boulevard des Invalides, where he settles in with his family.
Summer in Bavaria.
First exhibitions at New York ("291" Gallery), Moscow (Golden Fleece Salon) and Berlin (Cassirer Gallery).
Publishes "Notes of a Painter" in "La Grande Revue" of December 25.

1909 Summer at Cavalière.
First contract with Bernheim-Jeune.
Takes a house on the Route de Clamart, Issy-les-Moulineaux.

> 1909 Début of Diaghilev's Russian Ballet, at the Châtelet Theater, Paris.

1910 Retrospective at the Bernheim-Jeune Gallery.
At the Salon d'Automne, the two big decorations "Dance" and "Music" commissioned in the previous year by Shchukin.
With Marquet, visits the Exhibition of Islamic Art at Munich.
Spends winter in Andalusia.

> 1910 Rouault exhibition at Druet's.

1911 Works at Issy-les-Moulineaux. Summer at Collioure.
Short trip to Moscow in October.

> 1911 Foundation of "The Blue Rider" at Munich.
> Dufy designs textiles for Paul Poiret.
> Cubist rooms at the Indépendants and the Salon d'Automne.

1912 At Tangier until the spring.
First exhibition of his sculpture at the "291" Gallery, New York.
Returns to Morocco with Marquet and Camoin.

1913 On his return from Tangier, exhibition of the Moroccan pictures and of sculpture at the Bernheim Gallery (April).
Takes part in the Berlin "Secession" exhibition and in the "Armory Show" in New York, Chicago and Boston.

1914 Again takes a studio at 19, Quai Saint-Michel.
Exhibition at the Gurlitt Gallery, Berlin; Matisse's pictures confiscated as enemy property.
September at Collioure with Marquet and Juan Gris.

1915 Matisse Exhibition at Montross Gallery, New York, organized by Walter Pach.

1917 Summer at Chenonceaux with Marquet. Rejoins him at Marseilles in early winter. Falls ill and goes to Nice (Hôtel Beau-Rivage) to recuperate.
Renews his contract with Bernheim, who remains his dealer until 1926.

1918 Frequent visits to Renoir at Cagnes.
Moves to Hotel de la Méditerranée, Nice, on the Promenade des Anglais.
Exhibits with Picasso at the Paul Guillaume Gallery.

1918 Death of Guillaume Apollinaire.

1919 Exhibits regularly at the Bernheim Gallery (1919, 1920, 1922, 1923, 1924, 1927, 1929).
Exhibition in London at the Leicester Galleries.

1919 Death of Renoir.

1920 Designs sets and costumes for ballet "Le Rossignol," music by Igor Stravinsky, choreography by Leonide Massine, produced by Diaghilev's Ballets Russes.
Summer in London, then at Etretat.

1921 Summer at Etretat.
Moves into an apartment on Place Charles-Félix in the Old Town of Nice.

1924 Exhibition at the Brummer Galleries, New York.
Retrospective at the Ny Carlsberg Glyptothek, Copenhagen (preface by Leo Swane).

1925 Journey to Italy.

1927 First prize for painting at the Carnegie International Exhibition, Pittsburgh (he had already figured in the 1921, 1924, 1925 and 1926 exhibitions).

1928 Exhibition at Valentine Gallery, New York.

1930 Goes to Tahiti, via New York, San Francisco; returns by Suez.
Goes to Pittsburgh in the fall to serve on the jury of the Carnegie Exhibition, and to Merion where Dr Barnes commissions a mural on the theme of the "Dance."
Exhibition at Thannhauser Gallery, Berlin.

1930 Picasso awarded the Carnegie Prize.

1931 Returns to Nice to make the mural, and a set of etchings, commissioned by Albert Skira for "Poésies de Stéphane Mallarmé" (published 1932).
Exhibitions at Georges Petit Gallery, Paris; Kunsthalle, Basel; Museum of Modern Art, New York (preface by Alfred H. Barr).

1932 Second version of the "Dance."
Exhibition of the "Mallarmé" etchings at the Marie Harriman
Gallery, New York.

1932 Picasso Retrospective at Georges Petit Gallery.

1933 Final trip to Merion to install the "Dance."
On return journey stays at Venice and in the neighborhood.

1934 Pierre Matisse gives a series of exhibitions of his father's
work in his New York gallery: paintings (1934), the studies for
Shchukin's "Dance" (1936), paintings and drawings (1938),
paintings (1943), drawings (1945).

1935 Makes a tapestry cartoon, "Window at Tahiti," for Mme
Cuttoli.

1935 Death of Signac.

1936-1938 Annual exhibitions at Paul Rosenberg Gallery, Paris.

1937 Given a room at the exhibition "Maîtres de l'Art Indépendant,"
Petit-Palais, Paris.

1937 Picasso paints "Guernica."

1938 Moves into an apartment in the former Hotel Régina at Cimiez,
overlooking Nice.
Designs sets and costumes of the ballet "Rouge et Noir,"
music by Shostakovitch, choreography by Massine, produced
in 1939 by the Ballets Russes de Monte Carlo.
Matisse, Picasso, Braque exhibition at Oslo, Copenhagen and
Stockholm.

1941 Starts work on illustrations of "Florilège des Amours de
Ronsard," published by Skira in 1948, and those of Monther-
lant's "Pasiphaé," published by Fabiani in 1944.
Undergoes a serious operation for an intestinal occlusion in
Professor Leriche's clinic at Lyons.
Exhibition of recent graphic work at the Louis Carré Gallery,
Paris.

1943 Moves to the villa "Le Rêve" at Vence where he resides until
1948.

1943 Braque Retrospective at the Salon d'Automne.

1944 Begins the series of painted cut-and-pasted paper compositions figuring in "Jazz," published by Tériade in 1947.

1944 Picasso Retrospective at the Salon d'Automne.

1945 Retrospective in the "salle d'honneur" of the Salon d'Automne. Simultaneous one-man shows by Matisse and Picasso at the Victoria and Albert Museum, London (catalogue prefaced by C. Zervos); then at the Palais des Beaux-Arts, Brussels. Exhibition of six large canvases, with photographs of their successive states in the course of execution, at the Galerie Maeght, Paris.

1946 Cartoons for a two-piece tapestry, "Polynesia" (woven at the National Tapestry Factory, Beauvais, in 1948-1949). Illustrates "Love Letters of a Portuguese Nun" (Tériade) and Pierre Reverdy's "Visages" (Editions du Chêne).

1947 Elevated to the rank of Commander of the Legion of Honor. Exhibition of drawings at Liège.

1947 Death of Bonnard and Marquet.

1948 Retrospective at the Philadelphia Museum of Art. Devotes himself almost exclusively to planning the architecture and decoration of the Chapel of the Rosary, for the use of a chapter of Dominican nuns at Vence; it was consecrated on June 25, 1951, by Monseigneur Rémond, Bishop of Nice.

1948 Braque awarded the prize for painting at the XXIVth Biennale at Venice.

1949 Exhibition of large recent paintings at the Pierre Matisse Gallery, New York, then at the Musée d'Art Moderne, Paris (preface by Jean Cassou). Retrospective at Lucerne.

1950 Exhibition at the Galerie des Ponchettes, Nice (preface by Georges Salles), and at the Maison de la Pensée Française, Paris (preface by Louis Aragon, "Au Jardin de Matisse"). Awarded first prize for painting at the XXVth Venice Biennale. Exhibition at Milan and Rome (preface by Raymond Cogniat).

1951 Exhibition at the Museum of Modern Art, New York, then in Cleveland, Chicago and San Francisco.
Exhibition at the National Museum, Tokyo.

1951 Léger designs stained-glass windows for the church at Audincourt.

1952 Inauguration of the Musée Henri Matisse at Le Cateau-Cambrésis.
The Berggrüen Gallery, Paris, organizes a series of Matisse exhibitions devoted to recent graphic work (1952), cut-and-pasted papers (1953), rare lithographs (1954), unpublished drawings and sculptures (1958).

1952 Dufy wins first prize for painting at the XXVIth Venice Biennale.

1954 Death of Henri Matisse on November 3. He is buried in the cemetery at Cimiez, in a plot of ground offered by the city of Nice.

1956 Matisse Retrospective at the Musée d'Art Moderne, Paris (preface by Jean Cassou).

1958 Matisse Exhibition at the Bernheim-Dauberville Gallery, Paris (introduction by J. and H. Dauberville, "Une visite à Matisse en 1942").

1959 Exhibition of Matisse's last works, the large cut and pasted papers painted with gouache, at the Kunsthalle, Bern, then at the Stedelijk Museum, Amsterdam (1960), the Musée des Arts décoratifs, Paris (1961), the Museum of Modern Art, New York (1961), the Art Institute of Chicago (1962) and the San Francisco Museum of Art (1962).

1970 Matisse Centennial Exhibition at the Grand Palais, Paris, bringing together over 250 works.

MATISSE

AND HIS ŒUVRE

INTRODUCTION

OF all modern artists there is none regarding whom we have a documentation so abundant and authentic as is the case with Matisse. For in every period, at every stage of his career, he made a point of stating his exact intentions, whether in written articles or by word of mouth, choosing his words with an eye to clarity and precision. He said what to his thinking needed saying, and confined himself to essentials, but averse though he was from any sort of self-advertisement, he was always ready to reply at length to questions put him, doing his utmost to recall half-forgotten facts, to provide materials for an accurate chronology of his œuvre, and to further to the best of his ability the discovery of the truth and the whole truth about himself.

This willing co-operation facilitated research not only into the guiding principles of his art but also into the facts of his creative life, for Matisse was one of those rare, clear-sighted painters who do not shrink from scrutinizing in the dry light of reason their impulses, the sources of their inspiration, and setting forth what they find with total objectivity. Artists often profess an ignorance of the paths they followed in their initial quest of total self-expression; they would have us believe that they know nothing of what took place within them and leave this to their commentators to discover. This was not Matisse's way; he never ceased probing the mystery of the creative process and applied an intelligence far above the average to discovering the origins of his art, to analysing his means and to defining his aims. The effect of a commanding personality that he produced on visitors, as in earlier days on his fellow students, and then on his avant-garde colleagues, who were quick to recognize his superior intelligence and tenacity of purpose— this effect was fully justified, and his prestige accepted without demur. So we need not be surprised that appraisals of his art have usually been reiterations of statements made by the artist himself, and that the information given by those who were in touch with him relates chiefly to minor details, the overall view of his work being supplied or anyhow inspired by the master's personal declarations.

Needless to say, it would be absurd, not to say perverse, to leave out of account the light these declarations throw on the inner workings of a great creative mind. If there is any exception to the general rule that original artists are ill-equipped for evaluating the true significance of their innovations, Matisse was surely an exception to the rule. Yet, now that his life's work can be viewed in time's perspective, we are justified in re-examining its underlying structure, its curious felicities, and in drawing our own conclusions; nor need we accept without some reservations the mass of documentation brought together by Raymond Escholier in a work of nearly three hundred pages, mostly composed of the painter's personal remarks, statements by his friends and the many letters he exchanged with the former curator of the Petit Palais. To the wealth of information thus provided may be added the helpful comments we owe to the filial devotion of the artist's son, to the answers given by Matisse to detailed questionnaires, and to the authoritative studies by Alfred H. Barr and Gaston Diehl. Matisse himself believed (according to Georges Duthuit, who perhaps came nearer than any other to an intimate understanding of his personality) that no definitive character should be assigned to painters' "confessions" and *obiter dicta*, and that even their writings, often dashed off on the spur of the moment, should not be regarded as conclusive. As Matisse himself observed, "the artist puts the best of himself into his pictures; so much the worse for those for whom this is not enough; in the last analysis, what the artist *says* does not really matter much."

The present volume is an attempt to bring out, in the limited space at our disposal, the impressions that can be gleaned of Matisse's œuvre today, now that the commanding personality of the man who brought it into being is, alas, dwindling into a memory. And it seems to me that unqualified laudation would, like the hostile criticism of an earlier day, be inapt in dealing with a body of painting so diversified and still so brilliantly *alive*.

This œuvre, which spanned some sixty years and opened up so many new paths, is exacting, sometimes indeed austere, yet, while testifying to the artist's high intelligence and vigilant self-control, never lacks vivacity. At a quite early stage Matisse attained the level of the very greatest painters of the previous generation, but there were few to recognize this, since his major works of the time seemed calculated in so many cases to rebuff the eye of the beholder. How strict were the disciplines he then imposed on himself can be gauged when we remember the grace and beauty so delightfully distinctive of his later work.

An acute observer of the productions of the best of his contemporaries, Matisse was on familiar terms with some, but however great his attachment to his friends, he showed a curious reserve in his dealings with them; the art he was seeking to perfect could mature only in silence and aloofness. This is why, though in his early days he was regarded by his fellow students in Gustave Moreau's studio as their leading light, and though subsequently he proved himself an able and conscientious teacher, his name is not definitely linked up with any movement, even Fauvism, and he had no disciples. Yet he kept in touch with the vanguard art of his day, turned its innovations to account and frequently arrived at unexpected, masterly solutions of the very problems which seemed remotest from his personal preoccupations. Not limited to any group, his influence is widespread, if unobtrusive; few artists have done more than Matisse to shape the course of modern art.

SELF-PORTRAIT, 1900. CHARCOAL. MUSÉE HENRI MATISSE, LE CATEAU.

A LONG PATIENCE

1890-1903

IN Matisse we have one of the rare cases of a great artist quite unaware of his vocation until he passed the age of twenty; as a boy and youth, he showed no special interest in any form of art. But when the revelation came, it came so suddenly and overwhelmingly as to change the whole direction of his life. And he seems to have been conscious from the very start of his career that this "call," while conferring certain privileges, imposed on him, above all, obligations of no light order.

In the message he addressed to the townsfolk of Le Cateau-Cambrésis, his birthplace, on the occasion of the opening (November 8, 1952) of the local art museum consecrated to his work, Matisse described with admirable clarity and simplicity the circumstances of his crossing of the Rubicon—from nonentity to being, from uncertainty to certitude.

"Guided, I know not why, towards the path of Fine Art, and coming from a milieu which saw no reason to encourage me to follow it, I felt a 'call' to this form of activity, after having quite other plans for my future and, what is more, devoting several years to a very different occupation. After moving to Paris I spent a full year studying law at the University, without feeling a desire to visit any of our art museums, or even the yearly Salon de la Peinture, and I squandered my leisure time on the ordinary amusements of a young man of my age.

"Having secured the little diploma I had come to Paris to obtain, I returned to my provincial home and worked for several years in the office of a local lawyer. Then, in the course of a rather slow convalescence at Bohain, I took to copying the 'chromo' landscapes on the lid of a box of colors bought for me by my mother . . .

"During my schooldays at Saint-Quentin, at the Lycée Henri-Martin, I showed some talent in the elementary drawing class, as did my schoolfellow Emile Jean who, like me—though we never planned it out together or even dreamt of any such thing—found his way, later, to the Ecole des Beaux-Arts. It was largely due to chance that he and I joined forces, for we came from very different social backgrounds; as son of a school teacher, he may be said to have followed a natural bent; I, son of a grain merchant and originally intended to step into my father's shoes, was sidetracked, owing to my poor health, into a lawyer's office—which I left to enrol in the Beaux-Arts.

"Fully aware of the importance of the step I had decided on, and though I was convinced that this was my true vocation, the only one in which I could feel genuinely in my element and no longer the fish-out-of-water I had been in the lawyer's office, I took fright at first, knowing there could be no turning back. So I plunged headlong, blindly, into my new career, remembering a principle that had been drummed into me in boyhood and consisted of the two words 'Hurry up!' ... So, like my parents, I 'hurried up' with my work, impelled by a mysterious force which, I can see today, was quite foreign to my life as a 'normal' young man."

That period of childhood and youth is of interest since it helps to give an idea of the climate in which Matisse's personality took shape. All his life long he was remarkably sensitive to "atmospheres," and influenced by those with which he felt in harmony. He always had a sentimental attachment to the towns he had lived in as a boy, as is proved by his generosity towards the Museum and Infant School at Le Cateau. Bohain, where his parents lived, is a very ordinary small country town with narrow cobbled streets flanked by broad sidewalks of beaten earth. Le Cateau, where Matisse was born in the house of his grandfather, Gérard, who came of a long line of artisans, is a

town with much more character, thanks to the houses with oddly shaped façades that line its sloping public square, its charming Renaissance Town Hall and its belfry with a busy peal of bells, its church with a Baroque façade, and above all the stately Palais Fénelon, formerly the residence of the archbishops of Cambrai, with its handsome avenues of lindens. But, even more than by these buildings, I was impressed by the roads leading to this region of France and traversing it in all directions: especially the north roads driving straight ahead, hugging every rise of the ground and straddling the vast, wind-swept plain with unexpected switchbacks. And it struck me that Matisse's famous arabesque is, like them, a line that runs swiftly and surely to its goal and, with only the slightest deviations, brief arrests, hardly noticeable curves, succeeds in enclosing and comprising what, in the hands of other artists, would involve a host of digressions and detours.

The first of his paintings that Matisse judged "viable" dates from June 1890. This, the still life *Books and Candle*, which he never parted with, is a conscientious, carefully thought-out composition, an objective rendering of familiar objects closely observed and arranged quite simply; it has in short the modest value of a young man's experiment in a traditional technique. A year later, having overcome his father's opposition, he moved to Paris so as to devote himself entirely to his new vocation. This was the beginning of his "dark period" and he kept few of the works belonging to it except the figure studies subsequently presented to Le Cateau Museum. Having enrolled in the Académie Julian (then in the Faubourg Saint-Denis) where Bouguereau, Benjamin Constant and Gabriel Ferrier gave aspiring students a preparatory training for the Beaux-Arts, Matisse vainly struggled to bow to the disciplines of singularly uninspiring teachers, whom he always spoke of in after years with undisguised contempt. However, there was one bright spot;

Mat. 3

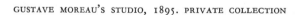

GUSTAVE MOREAU'S STUDIO, 1895. PRIVATE COLLECTION

in October 1892, at one of the evening classes of the Arts
Décoratifs, Matisse met Albert Marquet who was to be his
comrade in the years of struggle and a lifelong friend.

One day when he was drawing from casts of antique sculpture in the glass-enclosed court of the Ecole des Beaux-Arts,
Matisse caught the attention of Gustave Moreau, who was

inspecting the work of the students. Interested by Matisse's drawing, Moreau suggested that the young painter should join his class and even arranged for his being exempted from the entrance examination (March 1895). And now he had won his way into that famous studio, Matisse soon took courage to assert his personality. This was in fact the true beginning of his career; the young man rapidly advanced from strength to strength—and there can be no better evidence of the inspiring quality of Moreau's teaching in the last years of his life. Moreau's name is usually linked up with that of Rouault, who had an infinite respect for his great teacher and extolled his memory with almost filial devotion. Matisse was no less conscious of a debt to him, and Gaston Diehl has pointed out remarkable analogies between the aphorisms in which Moreau embodied the fruit of his meditations and profound technical knowledge, and the principles expounded by Matisse in his famous *Notes of a Painter* published December 25, 1908, in *La Grande Revue.*

Gustave Moreau attached more importance to a gymnastic of eye and mind than to the acquisition of manual dexterity; his view was that such skill, however adroitly employed, acquired its full value only when put to the service of a personal ideal. Basic to Moreau's teaching was a very real insight into the taste of the authentically great masters; and each of the students was left free to choose his favorites among them, then copy and "interpret" such of their works as he thought fit, always without regard to consecrated values. What the student had to do was, in a friendly rivalry discreetly suggested and encouraged by his teacher, to try to achieve that "pure" painting which stands for a happily inspired moment of communion between man and the universe; and at the same time to enter into and absorb the "atmosphere" of a given work—a Chardin still life, a Raphael portrait, a mythological scene by Poussin or a Ruisdael storm scene.

What strikes us most in these meticulously executed copies (many of which were, later, bought by the State and distributed to official buildings such as Grenoble Town Hall) is the extreme deference Matisse shows to his model. It was only somewhat later and in exceptional cases that he ventured on truly personal interpretations; and even in these he never indulged in the violent, arbitrary alterations practised by his friends Derain and Linaret. One gathers that his chief concern at this stage was to study and familiarize himself with *values*, and that what interested him above all was the making of a well-balanced composition that gave occasion for the placing and development of subtle effects of discreetly subdued light and modulations of the silvery tones dear to the Dutch masters. But considerable as was the technical proficiency he thus acquired, we must be careful not to overestimate the part played by these copies in the shaping of Matisse's talent. For even the original work he turned out during this early period seems oddly timid; a jolt from outside was needed to launch him on his appointed path.

Yet his admission to Gustave Moreau's studio had not only provided him with a certain mental and material security but brought him into contact with other talented young painters; for the first time he felt a self-assurance and a peace of mind thanks to which he could work steadily and rewardingly. While submitting conscientiously to the disciplines of the studio, he embarked on his own account on a series of carefully executed interiors and still lifes composed of objects all treated in much the same manner, with forms having little relief and rather dimly illuminated; in short, all the picture elements were subordinated to an ambience. The same uniformity of tones prevails in his early landscapes, painted in the course of a short stay in Brittany in the summer of 1895, and we also find it in Matisse's first showing at the Salon de la Société Nationale of April 1896 (five canvases, two of which were sold). That sensitive Flemish painter, Evenepoel, was quick to detect in his fellow student's work certain tendencies much like his own; in a letter written at the time, he described Matisse as "a delicate painter, very clever in his handling of greys."

Matisse did not try to isolate himself and he was made welcome by the older students, who were nearer him in age. When, some months later, the most conspicuous of these, Georges Rouault, who had been the moving spirit of the group, left the studio, Matisse made good his ascendancy over the newcomers, Flandrin, Camoin, Manguin and Linaret (Marquet joined them only in 1898).

The relations between Rouault and Matisse, the two outstanding members of the group, were almost certainly closer and more fruitful than has generally been supposed. Rouault kept throughout his life one of the largest and most significant of the male nudes in the series of figure studies painted by Matisse round about 1900, when he was at the Académie Carrière. Given to him by Matisse as a token of fraternal affection, this picture, with its strong, expressive distortions and strident colors—notably the blues and reds—has obvious analogies with the works Rouault himself was producing at the same time.

It would be interesting to trace the debt of the younger men of the period to the pioneer work of Vuillard, who was so bold an innovator in the layouts of his paintings of interiors, and had often employed themes resembling those of Matisse at this stage. Matisse, who was now beginning to frequent Durand-Ruel's gallery and Vollard's picture shop, studied with eager interest the works of the great Impressionists. But he was too modest to try to get in personal touch with those who were still alive. In later life he confessed that he never had the idea of going to see Cézanne, whom, however, he admired so intensely that, though he could ill afford it, he bought, in 1899 at Vollard's, the small Cézanne entitled *Three Bathers*.

Following the example of Manet (in his late still lifes dashed off with a superb brio), Matisse often inserted in his pictures areas of white—tablecloths or crockery—which served as light-traps in the center of the composition and gave scope for simple contrasts with black objects: a knife, a tall hat, an ebony frame or a dark bottle. In the summer of 1896 he was persuaded by

STILL LIFE WITH COFFEE POT, 1900. HERMITAGE, LENINGRAD.

Emile Wéry, a landscape painter who occupied a room adjoining his at 19, Quai Saint-Michel, to visit Belle-Ile-en-Mer, an island off the Breton coast. There they met John Russell, a friend of Rodin and Monet, who painted seascapes and landscapes with colored shadows in the impressionist manner, and collected work by Guillaumin, Emile Bernard and Van Gogh. (He later presented Matisse with two Van Gogh drawings.) His long stay in Belle-Ile, where he returned next summer, worked wonders with Matisse's art, filling it with the very breath of life. In his interior scenes objects and figures are suffused with an intense light that, flooding in through open doors and windows, gives them animation and substantiality. Though in the seascapes Matisse was now beginning to paint, the sea is always grey and gloomy, and though the forms of rocks are usually blurred by mist and rain, delightful passages of bright blue, delicate green and creamy white make their appearance in the pale Breton skies. For while these early seascapes are not yet free of the grisaille of his earlier work, Matisse has greatly brightened his palette. Large natural formations are clearly indicated: steep verticals of cliffs, luminous, vibrant horizontals of waves and beaches.

Matisse embodied all his new discoveries in a large canvas, the *Dinner Table*, completed in the winter of 1896-1897, and exhibited along with four still lifes at the 1897 Salon de la Nationale. Though it then had no success, it was hailed as a revelation when shown again in 1904, and rightly so. For it is a remarkable technical achievement, notable being the way in which tones are broken up and reciprocally influence each other, and the vivacity and sheen imparted to colors by light coming from different sources. Still there is no denying that the composition is governed by conventions of the past and the picture, for all its merits, strikes us as being rather a summing-up or terminal point of Matisse's 'prentice years than the dawn of a new period. Indeed it is diametrically opposed to the art he was to practise in the near future. This extreme refinement, this piling up of details that even overflow the margin of the picture, these strained effects and hankering after perfect "finish"—all these he was now to turn his back on peremptorily and definitively. The ill-success of the *Dinner Table* was in fact a blessing in disguise. Having realized that the technical means he had mastered should not be brought into prominence but discreetly put to the service of a higher end—that of a synthetic pictorial architecture, thought out afresh for every composition—Matisse was now to make what was nothing short of a new start.

Sponsored by Russell, who had already introduced him to Rodin, Matisse paid several visits to Pissarro, who gave him a friendly welcome and much helpful advice, pointing out, amongst other things, apropos of the *Dinner Table*, that one does not produce the effect of light with white. One of their conversations has been recorded verbatim by Georges Duthuit.

"What is an Impressionist?" Matisse asked Pissarro.

"He is a painter who never paints the same picture twice over; all his pictures are different."

"For example?"

"Sisley. Cézanne is not an Impressionist. He is a classical artist because whether he painted women bathing, Mont Sainte-Victoire or similar subjects, he painted the same picture all his life long. Cézanne never painted sunlight—only grey days."

"In other words," Matisse, who at fifty years' distance remembered every word that was said, explained to Duthuit, "Cézanne's sensations are always sensations of cloudy weather."

Matisse was now about to "discover" the light of the South, and the conversation quoted above has its significance in this context. It was at the beginning of 1898, just after his marriage, that he decided to leave Paris for a year and devote himself entirely to personal creative work. After a short trip to London to look at the Turners, he left for Corsica. "It was at Ajaccio," he told Raymond Escholier, "that I had my revelation of the South, which I now saw for the first time." Life in Corsica delighted him and he prolonged his stay for six months. It was here that he attuned his vision to that Mediterranean light which, from Collioure to St Tropez, from Tangier to Vence and Nice, was henceforth to be the natural "climate" of his art.

Pure color now made a dramatic appearance in his compositions, no longer as an exception but as an all-over technique whose possibilities he tested out in various types of pictures.

In his interiors, where blazing sunlight, framed in doors and windows, brings out shadows much as the surrounding heat stresses the coolness of the room, the tones are charged with deep vibrations played off against each other to wonderful effect. We find this in *The Invalid* (Cone Collection, Baltimore Museum), in which the main theme emerges at a certain distance from the spectator—if nearer, it would merely create an effect of confusion —out of a mass of violently brushed-on strokes of different lengths, charged with rich, unctuous pigment. Here, all essential elements are stressed; the arm lying on the blanket is boldly extended, its length being emphasized by fringes of bright color, forms are overlapped by the all-pervading light and, when these tend to heighten the expressive power of the presentment, the artist introduces rhythms irrelevant to the factual description of objects. Matisse rings the changes on vertical and horizontal strokes, indifferently; it is as if he were feverishly straining after some effect never completely realized. Yet the general impression given by *The Invalid* is not that of a sketch but of a fully developed work, though it leaves us with a feeling that the artist deliberately held his hand, without troubling about "finish" or exactitude, so as to ensure the picture's maximum intensity.

In his open-air scenes, the flooding light tends to attenuate the impact of the colors, making them more subdued and

THE INVALID, 1899. CONE COLLECTION, BALTIMORE MUSEUM OF ART.

A GLIMPSE OF NOTRE-DAME IN THE LATE AFTERNOON, 1902.
ALBRIGHT-KNOX ART GALLERY, BUFFALO, N.Y.

limiting the proliferations of the strokes. During his frankly experimental phase in Corsica, then in the six months he spent in the neighborhood of Toulouse, Matisse progressively fined down his subjects to their simplest elements—almost, one might say, to their minor elements, were it not that he invested even the least of these with a curious majesty, an almost epic grandeur. A lonely tree in a wheatfield, a clump of small olive trees, the white front of a house, a sunlit courtyard, the greenery of a secluded garden—such were the themes of these moments of ecstatic vision, pictured in all their plenitude, yet without ever overtaxing the resources of the medium. It has been said that in this period Matisse was trying out the procedures of Impressionism, including (in a purely empirical manner) the Neo-Impressionist theories then being promulgated by Paul Signac in his articles in *La Revue Blanche* (May to July 1898)—first version of a work that was destined to become a classic of its kind. But though he sometimes employed the dot technique, this was never done systematically and its object was not so much to "atomize" color as to evoke space. Matisse's innovations were invariably simple, direct and wholly personal; one gets the impression that he deliberately refrained from profiting by the discoveries of his immediate predecessors. For it was instinctive with him always to strike out in new directions, making, if needed, a series of fresh starts, so as to reach the point at which he aimed by short-cuts discovered by himself.

By the time he settled into his stride on his return to Paris, so great was the gap between the stage he now had reached and the art in vogue there, that he felt obliged, cost what it might materially speaking, to cut his last links with the Ecole des Beaux-Arts, with the official salons (which in any case would have closed their doors to him) and even with the Louvre to which none of the great moderns—Cézanne, Seurat, Van Gogh and Gauguin—had as yet won admission.

It was now that Matisse and Marquet became firm friends, and the two of them devoted much time to sketching from life. Marquet had already become an expert in this field; indeed his life drawings made on the spot displayed a fine precision and an economy of means ranking him beside the most skillful artists of the Far East. Matisse, too, tried his hand at instantaneously recording the bare essentials of everyday scenes and figures, and his drawings in Indian ink, though lacking the wit and subtlety of Marquet's, have that structural solidity which he was soon to impart to his work in colors. When they painted side by side in the Luxembourg gardens, in the streets of Arcueil or, from high windows overlooking the Quai Saint-Michel, made views in bird's-eye perspective of the bridges and Notre-Dame, it was Matisse who was the guiding spirit, and he had little trouble in persuading his friend to follow up the discoveries he himself had made during his stay in the South.

Seeking to recapture under the softer skies of Paris a light that exalts forms instead of drowning and dissolving them, he had no scruples about stepping up colors to an extreme intensity corresponding to an ideal vision far more vivid than the normal. Two ways for this lay open, and he explored them simultaneously. Either a sheet of orange-tinted flame gradually submerged objects, blotting out surface differences, but pitted here and there with dark recesses, last vestiges as it were of a world in fusion. (This is notably the case with the big still lifes in which Matisse, abandoning the complexity of his earlier compositions, confined himself to a few basic, isolated elements viewed frontally or in slightly oblique recession.) Alternatively, expelling dark colors from his palette, he had recourse to a dovetailed pictorial construction in sober yet eye-filling colors, all planes being demarcated by thick contour lines. Even the most lavishly colored works of this period are held together by this architectonic ordering of the picture content, and,

THE PATH IN THE BOIS DE BOULOGNE, 1902.
PUSHKIN MUSEUM OF FINE ART, MOSCOW.

reciprocally, the most severely ordered compositions are vitalized by the freshness and novelty of Matisse's color schemes. Already present in his work was that distinctive quality—a rare combination of stability and flexibility—which he himself elucidated towards the close of his life, in the text accompanying *Jazz*. "The plumbline, giving as it does the vertical, supplies

MALE MODEL (ATELIER CARRIÈRE), 1900. PRIVATE COLLECTION, PARIS.

together with its opposite, the horizontal line, the draftsman's coordinates. The vertical is present in my mind; it helps me to define the direction of the other lines . . . I never draw a curve, for example a branch in a landscape, without bearing in mind its relation to the vertical."

His next task was to integrate the human figure—that vertical *par excellence*—into the world he was creating and with a view to solving the problems this presented, Matisse took to frequenting a humble studio on the Rue de Rennes where Eugène Carrière sometimes dropped in to correct the young men's work. None of Moreau's former students came there, but there was a group of newcomers, Jean Puy, Laprade, Derain, Chabaud and Biette. When the Académie Carrière closed, the group clubbed together to hire a model and worked in Biette's studio. Matisse much impressed the other members of the group by a brilliant series of figure studies which displayed a marked advance in his handling of colors and pictorial construction. These figures look as if they were hacked out with an ax, their contours are stressed by black lines, lateral planes are marked by touches of pure vermilion or emerald green, while cobalt blue, carmine and pink are worked into the flesh tints. They are posed in such a way as to show the model's muscular development to full advantage, and almost give the impression of rough-hewn statues. During this period Matisse frequently attended the municipal school on the Rue Etienne-Marcel, where there was a studio for sculpture, and it was there that he made a powerful free copy of Barye's *Jaguar devouring a Hare*, "identifying himself with the frenzy of the wild beast, as expressed by the rhythmic movement of the masses."

WOMAN WITH THE HAT, 1905.
COLLECTION MR AND MRS WALTER A. HAAS.

THE "CONDENSATION OF SENSATIONS"

1903-1911

His recourse to the disciplines of sculpture was, to begin with, regarded by Matisse as merely complementary to his experiments in painting. In sculpture he allowed himself a wider freedom and also showed more perseverance, sometimes devoting months or even years to bringing out the essential qualities of a subject by a process of simplification and elimination. Also he applied himself to discovering the best ways of expressing volume by synthetic curves and by integrating movement into forms, ruthlessly eliminating every trace of the accidental and superfluous. Rodin had advised him to study the members of the body as separate units, and in *The Slave* (1900-1903) Matisse went so far as to suppress the arms of the figure which thus acquires far greater expressiveness thanks to the accentuation of the torso resting on the splayed-out limbs, while similarly the bulge of shoulders and shoulder blades emphasizes the hollow of the chest. There are obvious affinities between *The Slave* and the nudes Matisse painted at the Académie Carrière. We find a similar approach in the *Madeleine* (1901), where the folded arms seem welded to the languorously swaying figure. Matisse shows less inventiveness when he takes to representing on canvas figures with accentuated volumes, surrounded by accessories and decorative elements. We must not forget that by this time the excitement of his first contacts with the South had worn off, and he now was passing through a phase both of material difficulties and of misgivings, which led him to revert to more literal renderings of appearance, in drab, muted colors. And though he tried his best to regain that first fine rapture in sketches made in the open air, in Switzerland (where he joined his parents in 1901), the time at his disposal was too limited.

For he usually needed a certain lapse of time for his immediate impressions to bear fruit. Nor was he any more successful with the sketches he made in the Bohain countryside, which he revisited on several occasions.

Actually the value of Matisse's ventures into sculpture is much less evident when these works were treated merely as rehearsals for his paintings, than when they served to open his eyes to new domains of art. In the latter case they acted as a salutary counterpoise, sometimes even an antidote when, no longer yielding to the promptings of instinct, he applied himself to deliberately trying out the possibilities of color; that is to say after he met Signac and became acquainted with the doctrines of Neo-Impressionism. 1904 was the crucial year in this respect. It began by a sort of stock-taking of his work of recent years. He exhibited six canvases at the Indépendants and had his first one-man show in June at Vollard's. This comprised forty-six works: most of the landscapes painted at Belle-Ile, at Arcueil and Bohain, in Corsica, Switzerland and Paris, as well as the chief still lifes of the last ten years. Then, at the Salon d'Automne, he exhibited fourteen paintings and two sculptures. Meanwhile, however, he was striking out in new directions; he had been to St Tropez, where he spent the summer with Signac and Cross, whose friendly counsels did much to orient his course in the near future.

For Matisse's new encounter with the Mediterranean scene did not take place in solitude as formerly, but in the company of artists who were both theoreticians and masters of their craft, and with whom he now was qualified to exchange ideas to their mutual advantage. The first canvases of this phase—for example, *The Terrace, St Tropez* (Isabella Stewart Gardner Museum, Boston)—are a direct homage to the beauty of the landscape and the glorious luminosity of the atmosphere, which had cast their spell on him once more. And he now made haste to systematize his means in the light of the ingenious, would-be scientific theories his new friends had built up on premises laid down by Seurat. Later on, Matisse frankly confessed (to Tériade and Gaston Diehl amongst others) how disappointed he was with his first attempts in this direction and how reluctant he was to keep to hard-and-fast rules whose effect would have been to "mutilate" his colors in compliance with the "laws" of modulated tones—while all the time his instinct was urging him to step them up and indulge in vigorous contrasts. All the same it seems that, without ever being a wholly orthodox Pointillist, Matisse succeeded in assimilating all that served his turn in a doctrine that enabled him to liberate his palette to dazzling effect. Even in the work of the Neo-Impressionists we can see a sharp distinction between their large, carefully planned compositions, often a little cold and arbitrary, and their watercolors dashed off effortlessly with brilliant sleight of hand. This experimental phase was all the more beneficial since Matisse always reacted in a quite personal manner to his friends' ideas; not only does the linear structure make its presence felt beneath the shimmering play of colors, but the colors actually tend to reinforce it. Similarly his sense of mass and sculpturesque form was unimpaired by the dispersal of the planes, and he refused to impose on his color—invariably simple and forceful—any over-subtle modulations; on the contrary, he maintained its dominants and contrasts. And this constructive line which meant so much to Matisse, holding its own, an Ariadne's clew, across the haze of broken lights, was to become that colored arabesque which in the following year confirmed his high originality.

Even in the mythological allegories, in the nymphs and fauns with which Cross and Signac now were peopling their pictures, Matisse found helpful sources of inspiration, so aptly did they fit into the ambience of the "earthly paradise" he was now discovering on the shores of the Mediterranean and which was henceforth to haunt his creative imagination. For he had no need, like Gauguin, to seek it over-sea; he found all he wanted in the St Tropez countryside and bay, in its curving beach, its olive groves and, at the end of the pinewoods, a single, tall, upstanding tree, stabilizing the composition. Now he had decided on the basic elements of his picture, he applied himself

STUDY FOR "LUXE, CALME ET VOLUPTÉ," 1904.
COLLECTION OF AMBASSADOR AND MRS JOHN HAY WHITNEY, NEW YORK.

to grouping them within a vast synthetic composition, including a number of nude figures which, while representing contemporary women bathers on a beach, carried mythical overtones answering to Baudelaire's famous triad: *Luxe, calme et volupté.* The small preparatory study reproduced (John Hay Whitney Collection, New York) is built up with short, irregular touches fusing into accents and heightening the impact of the colors. This was followed by a full-size picture, made in the artist's studio on his return to Paris, which had the air of a declaration of faith in the tenets of Neo-Impressionism, with its mosaic of somewhat subdued colors and its ordered structure based on a subtle rhythm of alternating verticals and curves. Signac was so much struck by it that he gave it a place of honor in the 1905 Salon des Indépendants, bought it and took it to his villa at St Tropez, where it hung undisturbed on a wall of his dining room for the next forty years; it is now in Madame Ginette Signac's Collection in Paris. This picture was the subject of heated comments in the press and discussions among artists. "Once I'd seen this picture," Dufy told his biographer, "I understood all the new principles of painting, and impressionist realism lost its charm for me as I contemplated this miracle of the imagination introduced into design and color."

After being appointed (through the good offices of Signac) chairman of the hanging committee of the Indépendants, Matisse, in virtue of his functions, played a large part in the big Seurat and Van Gogh retrospective exhibitions which were outstanding features of the 1905 Salon. There is little doubt that these close contacts with the works of the two masters were beneficial. In both the sketches and the large-scale compositions of Seurat, first to affirm the unity and homogeneity of the flat surface of the canvas, he found a brushstroke persistently vibrant and mobile, with nothing arbitrary or mechanical about it, charged with flickering gleams and subtle nuances, yet retaining unimpaired, despite the ever-changing play of light, its initial color. In an atmosphere of calm and perfect balance the rich complexity of Seurat's composition unfurled itself, serenely ordered, while his masterly design imposed an organic unity on the whole. As for Van Gogh, he had achieved his personal style only after passing through a divisionist phase which led him to introduce light into his color. Matisse found in the works of the two masters justifications for his personal interpretation of an art theory whose procedures he had thoroughly explored but from which he had made haste to jettison anything that in the least resembled a set formula. Yet he could not fail to recognize that in it he had found permanent and comprehensive laws for the organization of the picture —all-pervasive rhythms, just balance and harmony—and these would help him to fulfill on his own account the program Félix Fénéon had suggested to his friends (while Seurat was still alive) when he said that their discoveries would lead the way to "a great development on decorative lines."

Whereas Marquet, Camoin and Manguin elected to spend their summer vacation at the now familiar St Tropez, Matisse's choice fell on one of the remotest and most rugged corners of the French Catalonian coast. The little fishing port of Collioure provided him with a self-contained natural setting, a brief stretch of sea flanked by brightly colored rocks. From the very start Matisse brought off some brilliantly successful compositions executed with happy spontaneity, in which small, separate strokes (now slightly elongated) at once created an overall rhythm and built up rock formations of a remarkable solidity. And he foresaw that this change in his technique was of a momentous order; he was moving away from pointillist "atomization" towards flat tracts of smoothly applied color. His palette noticeably brightened and in his views of the village, with pink or ochreous tones predominating, as in his interior

PASTORAL, 1905. MUSÉE DU PETIT-PALAIS, PARIS.

scenes flooded with brilliant light streaming in through open windows, Matisse gave free rein to his sense of delight in all creation, *le bonheur de vivre*.

This, the *Joy of Life*, was to be the title of the big work he was now to embark on, an arcadian, timeless synthesis of all the impressions he had gathered in that memorable summer and

45

Mat. 13

SKETCH FOR "THE JOY OF LIFE," 1905.
COLLECTION MR AND MRS WALTER A. HAAS.

their summing up—in the same way as *Luxe, calme et volupté* had been a crystallization of his discoveries of the previous year. But this time Matisse imposed the stamp of his personality on the scene, and so masterfully that it acted as a revelation and a lesson—in the first instance to Derain (whom he had invited to Collioure on his return from military service) and a little later to Friesz. There was now no real difference in kind between the many sketches dashed off on the spur of the moment in the neighboring countryside—finest of which is the *Pastoral* in the Petit-Palais—and their vast, monumental transposition into the great work he painted in his studio during the winter in view of the 1906 Salon des Indépendants, and in

LANDSCAPE AT COLLIOURE, 1906. HERMITAGE, LENINGRAD.

which he gave superb expression to the pantheist dream of a world of joy untrammelled. It is clear how vast a distance has been covered when we note all that the painter's imagination has added to the basic facts of day-by-day observation and how these are exalted by master-rhythms deriving from the essential themes. This picture (Barnes Foundation, Merion, where to our regret permission to photograph it in color has not been granted) is, perhaps, Matisse's supreme work; more even than *Luxe, calme et volupté*, it would have justified Dufy's enthusiastic approbation (cited above). Here Matisse has passed beyond Pointillism, light is fused into colors accented by their complementaries, planes being suggested by ever-changing convolutions of the arabesque. The groups of figures are spaced out in an atmosphere of translucent shadows (Derain has noted that at Collioure shadow is never opaque, but "a whole world of clarity and luminosity"). Whether stationary or in motion, these groups are transversed by an overall pulsation, the vital rhythm of nature herself, and together form as it were a paradisial harmony. The setting plays a part in this effect, though it does not answer to any identifiable scene, being an amalgam of many varieties of scenery—woodlands, beaches, sea and sky blended into an ideal backdrop, the landscape of a dream.

This décor became more and more simplified, reduced to a near-abstract colored ground, when Matisse, following up his idea to its logical conclusion, harked back to the figures and groups of the big picture, and treated them individually, developing their utmost possibilities and breathing into them a yet intenser life. The *Blue Nude* (1907, Cone Collection, Baltimore Museum of Art), in which are reminiscences of a brief visit to Biskra in Algeria the year before, has a somewhat composite character due to the intrusion of such exotic elements as mauve and pink palm leaves with green ribs. But what strikes us most is the curious transformation of the woman's figure effected by the black contour lines and blue shadows. There is also an expressive exaggeration of the domes of the hip and breasts and, in contrast with this, a sort of whittling down of the face and the areas of luminous flesh, somewhat similar in effect to Goya's drastic treatment of the figure in the *Maja Desnuda*.

In *Le Luxe I*, painted at Collioure in 1907 (Musée d'Art Moderne, Paris), the figures are brought into closer harmony with the supporting ground. But in the second version (J. Rump Collection, Statens Museum, Copenhagen), painted in winter 1907-1908, of the same dimensions and having the same subject,

THE BLUE NUDE, 1907. BALTIMORE MUSEUM OF ART, CONE COLLECTION.

LE LUXE I, 1907. MUSÉE D'ART MODERNE, PARIS.

the variations and modulations of color differentiating the figures according to their attitudes and respective distances from the spectator, have completely disappeared, as have the skillfully constructed transitional passages between the distant prospects, sea and mountains, clouds and blue sky. Here everything is rendered in areas of flat, local color which equalize the values

THE GAME OF BOWLS, 1908. HERMITAGE, LENINGRAD.

THE DANCE, 1910. HERMITAGE, LENINGRAD.

of the three figures and the clearly demarcated landscape elements. In the *Game of Bowls* (1908, Hermitage, Leningrad) and *Bathers with a Turtle* (1908, Joseph Pulitzer Jr. Collection, St. Louis) backgrounds are reduced to schematic horizontal bands. Distinctive of these variations on the theme of a trio of male or female figures is the artist's use of a firm, decided line and bold, remarkably effective foreshortenings; nor has he demurred at introducing into each of the paintings a "shock" element; in one the vivid patch of color formed by the turtle

MUSIC, 1910. HERMITAGE, LENINGRAD.

at the women's feet, and in the other the vermilion wrap around the standing youth. Besides these two striking figure compositions, a number of sketches of the same period, representing musicians, women dancing or bathing, their movements stressed by the heavy black contour line, testify to the artist's ambition to achieve a sort of sublimated Purism (as is, indeed, suggested by his use of the word "purity" on several occasions).

Matisse now formed a project for the creation of a series of large decorations, and he outlined his intentions to a journalist friend, Estienne (see *Les Nouvelles*, April 12, 1909). "Suppose I wish to decorate a studio. There are three floors, let's say. I picture a visitor coming in from the street. The first thing he sees is the ground floor. Here what's needed is to give him something calling at once for an effort and also giving a feeling of relaxation. So my first panel represents the *Dance*, a group of figures circling up above a hill. On the second floor we are in the heart of the house, where all is silence, pensive meditation. Here I picture a scene of music-making with attentive listeners. Then, on the third floor, all is peace; I paint some people lying on the grass, engaged in talk or lost in dreams. This I propose to do by the simplest and fewest possible means—for it is eminently these that enable a painter to figure forth his inner vision in its entirety." He went on to list these means. "Three colors for a big panel devoted to the *Dance*; the blue of the sky, the pink of the bodies, the green of the hillside." And summing up his program: "We move towards serenity by a simplification of ideas and plastic values. The *ensemble* is our sole ideal." As it so happened, he had just received, after long discussions and negotiations, a commission from Shchukin to paint two large companion pictures, the *Dance* and *Music*, which were to decorate, not an "ideal studio," but the staircase of the 18th-century palace in Moscow owned by the great Russian collector. And it was under this form that Matisse, while keeping scrupulously faithful to the means he had enjoined upon himself, carried out his project.

Efforts have been made to trace the origins of the group of figures of the *Dance*, which in the *Joy of Life* had been located on a sea beach in the distance, but now straddles a hilltop whose curves are wedded to its rhythm. Matisse himself was always evasive when questioned on the subject—was it a reminiscence of the "farandoles" he had seen in Montmartre in his youth, or of the "sardagnes" of Collioure?—and actually there is nothing in this grandiose vision to link it up with such trivial antecedents. What Matisse has bodied forth is the "Idea" of the Dance, conceived as a rite transcending the local and ephemeral; the forms of the dancers are not merely those of human bodies in motion, but the *essential* forms of rhythmic movement, impetuous yet measured speed, the elemental undulations of the waves of the sea. And the three intensely saturated colors (the least change would mar their absolute perfection) form as it were a chord of music—a quintessence of all color.

Matisse's second composition, *Music*, presented greater difficulties, being based not on an all-over movement but on an equilibrium of compactly posed, stationary bodies, arranged like notes on a stave of music. The general opinion that *Music* is "inferior" to the *Dance*—Shchukin used this as a pretext for paying less for it—is not, in my opinion, justified.

While Matisse thus succeeded in bringing to life the "figure-in-itself" by investing it with all the attributes of a living being, he also, by a converse process, mastered the rendering of the individualized face, doing justice both to its universal qualities and to personal traits—in a word its "likeness." Hitherto he had been relatively little interested in portraiture. The most he did was to make studies of his own reflected face in drawings showing it in three-quarter view, the eyebrow widely raised above a big square eye. When for the *Guitarist* (1903, Ralph F. Colin Collection, New York) he had his wife pose in Spanish costume, what he chiefly aimed at was a *generalized* depiction of the figure. At Collioure he tried out a new method when, seated, face to face, he and Derain made each other's portraits. Recently acquired by the Tate Gallery, these two works are well worth comparing. In that of Derain, who employed a technique of schematically arranged patches and arbitrary transpositions of color, we find more ease and virtuosity, and some have held that in this branch of art he

GIRL IN GREEN, 1909. HERMITAGE,
LENINGRAD.

SPANISH DANCER, 1909.
PUSHKIN MUSEUM OF FINE ART, MOSCOW.

influenced Matisse. The fact remains, however, that the latter's portrait is more effective, such is the flexibility of the brushstrokes, which prolong the datum of immediate perception, and such the dynamism of the color.

In this new field he was exploring Matisse acquired a rapid mastery, as is evidenced by various portraits of his wife, his

SCULPTURE AND PERSIAN VASE, 1908. NATIONAL GALLERY, OSLO.

daughter and himself. The *Woman with the Hat* (Mr and Mrs Walter A. Haas Collection, San Francisco) created a considerable scandal, perhaps because the public saw something almost sacrilegious in its treatment of a then fashionable theme, when it was exhibited at that famous Salon d'Automne of 1905 where the term "Fauvism" was coined. (In this context it may be pointed out that, as against the usual view that the inventor of the name was the critic Louis Vauxcelles who, on observing an inoffensive statuette by Marque placed in the middle of the gallery where the "revolutionaries" were hung, exclaimed, "*Ah! Donatello au milieu des fauves!*"—as against this legend Rouault always maintained that it was Matisse who, when seen entering the gallery wearing a shaggy overcoat, provoked the exclamation, "*Tiens, voilà les fauves!*") Compared with the *Woman with the Hat*, which somehow does not carry entire conviction, since the effect of the face itself, despite the heightened color and the skillful marbling of the flesh tints, is weakened by the chromatic violence of the dress and the huge, garish superstructure of the hat, that other famous portrait, the *Green Stripe* (J. Rump Collection, Statens Museum, Copenhagen), seems far more significant, such is its simplicity and so elegant are the pure tones painted flat without transitions. A broad green stripe runs down the face dividing it into two symmetrical zones of color, one cool, the other warm; one edged with rose, the other with green. Also, this portrait tells much about the sitter's personality; nothing could be more revealing than this long, determined, pensive face and its forthright gaze. This second work shows a distinct advance on its predecessor—but one of which Matisse, it seems, did not take account immediately, since in the following year we find him still hesitating between two tendencies, one representing the expressionist climate of art prevailing at the time, and the other his deeper, perhaps truer instincts. Thus it was in 1906 that he painted the most outrageously "fauve" of all his canvases, *The Gypsy* (Musée de l'Annonciade, St Tropez) whose curious grimace is due to an almost extravagant disdain of form and a riotous profusion of reds and greens. Fortunately this seems to have been no more than a flash in the pan; when we turn to the *Self-Portrait* of the same year (J. Rump Collection, Statens Museum, Copenhagen), we cannot fail to be struck by its hieratic dignity, the firmness of the drawing, the nobility of the attitude, and the controlled organization of the nuances and modulations out of which emerges the face lightly shaded with green. The delightful *Marguerite Reading* (1906, Grenoble), treated with the same fine control, is a portrait on almost classical lines, in which Matisse seems to have resisted that urge to dissonance which had led him to so many bold experiments with color; here we have a young girl bending over an open book, the face defined by a few well-marked lines and telling out against a background tinged with blue and pink.

The two versions of *The Young Sailor* (Private Collection, Norway, and Private Collection, Chicago) were painted at Collioure in the summer of 1906 with only a few days' interval between; here we see Matisse moving on from an angular design, emphasized by the play of complementaries, to a rendering in which the contour line is fused into areas of flat color which, adjusted to a rhythm of flowing curves, indicate the figure's attitude and movement. To simplify the juxtaposition of violent colors, without the use of circumscribing lines, the artist has left some passages of white canvas between them (cf. *Pink Onions*, 1906, J. Rump Collection, Statens Museum, Copenhagen). Before long, however, he took to frankly placing the colors side by side, but he arranged them so adroitly that they fall naturally into place, without jarring the eye, as in *Still Life with Melon* (Barnes Foundation, Merion) and the gorgeous *Oriental Rugs* (Sembat Collection, Grenoble Museum) in which the dominant hue of red is skillfully allied with cool, clear harmonies of green

and brown. Thus after having for so long felt called on to
demarcate his colors by heavy bounding lines, thick as the
cames of stained-glass windows, or by playing them off against
complementaries or passages of shadow, Matisse had now
acquired such proficiency that all he needed was to lay on the

THE DINNER TABLE (HARMONY IN RED), 1908. HERMITAGE, LENINGRAD.

Mat. 24

COFFEE POT, CARAFE AND FRUIT DISH, 1909.
HERMITAGE, LENINGRAD.

desired color at the appropriate place, and the mere fact of its presence there gave it its full, distinctive value and significance.

As a result of persistent experimentation, Matisse arrived at an extreme concision—"all that is not useful in the picture is harmful," he wrote in the famous article in the *Grande Revue* of December 1908—and a sense of the value of abridgement.

STILL LIFE WITH A GERANIUM, 1910.
BAYERISCHE STAATSGEMÄLDESAMMLUNG, MUNICH.

In the portrait of Marguerite (owned by Picasso) and that of Madame Matisse, the *Red Madras Headdress* (Barnes Foundation, Merion), such is the suggestive power of the colored line—acting as a schematic résumé of the picture content—that it not only serves to demarcate the areas of flat color but brings out their significance as constructive elements. And, again, in the

63

large half-length figures of 1909 and 1910, the *Girl in Green* and the *Girl with Tulips* (Hermitage Leningrad), it is the line that organizes the picture surface into a telling counterpoint of plenitudes and intensities. Here the personal characteristics of the model are translated into a "universal" language, at once ascetic and elementary. The dynamism of the line is further stressed by the use of black when Matisse is concerned with exotic subjects such as the *Algerian Woman* (Musée d'Art Moderne, Paris) and the *Spanish Dancer* (Pushkin Museum of Fine Art, Moscow)— new themes in handling which Matisse does not as yet range beyond their more obvious implications.

Nonetheless he manipulates color with an unprecedented freedom, dematerializes it, deprives it of any utilitarian or imitative function; everywhere it is governed solely by the patterning of the picture surface and modified accordingly— provided always that the overall balance of the composition is not disturbed by vagaries of the color scheme. When invited to give at the Salon d'Automne of 1908 a viewing of his most recent work (eleven paintings, thirteen sculptures and some drawings), he included a large decorative panel intended for Sergei Shchukin's dining room. In this Matisse reverted to the theme of the early *Dinner Table (La Desserte)* but changed it out of recognition, since the picture elements were here projected on to a completely flat surface and the whole comprised a "Harmony in Blue." Some months later, however, he sent to Russia a panel identical in composition but entirely repainted; this was the *Harmony in Red*, now in the Hermitage, Leningrad. (Here we have the first instance of what was to become a constant practice with Matisse, that of trying out a work in successive states until he arrived at a version that completely satisfied him.) Three-quarters of the picture consists of a flat red ground; the same material, patterned with large blue decorative motifs picked out with black, covers both the wall and the table

THE MANILA SHAWL (MADAME MATISSE), 1911.
RUDOLF STAECHELIN COLLECTION, BASEL.

(which is rendered in "folded-back" planes), making both tablecloth and wall into a vertical expanse of red. For depth is completely abolished and still-life objects are reduced to a few isolated patches, hardly more than signs, while the figure on the right is a mere silhouette filling a crevice of the backdrop. The grandiose simplicity Matisse has achieved in this large decorative work is emphasized by the arabesque of motifs animating the vast monochrome surfaces.

Before continuing on the new, auspicious path which this picture, first of a brilliant lineage, had opened up, Matisse painted a series of still lifes which, for all their high qualities, conformed to some extent with conventions of the past. All the same he succeeded in solving several problems that had hitherto perplexed him. Thus, in several instances, he places in his compositions statuettes he has just finished; he seems to feel that, better than living models, they suggest rotundity and volume. It is as if he were seeking to integrate another dimension into the surface by means of artifacts which, having already been transposed from nature, had acquired a plasticity and substantiality of a superior order. For example, the *Sleeping Nude* of 1907, which reproduces in sculpture the violent distortions of the *Blue Nude*, is used as a *point de repère* for the coloristic intensity of *Sculpture and Persian Vase* (1908, National Gallery, Oslo) and also sets the scale of the picture. The *Sleeping Nude*, presented frontally and in full light, figures again in *Goldfish* (1909, J. Rump Collection, Statens Museum, Copenhagen), where it creates an impression of depth in terms of verticality. In *Still Life with a Red Commode* (1910, Moscow) the statuette has become transparent and been integrated into the flat surface of the picture. Statuettes appear in other pictures, but incidentally, as casual objects, merged into the sumptuous décor; the *Two Negresses* of 1908, for example, figures in *Fruit and Bronze* (Pushkin Museum, Moscow). In several still lifes we have

Mat. 27

instances of Matisse's overriding concern with *surface* during this period. In *Coffee Pot, Carafe and Fruit Dish* (1909, Hermitage, Leningrad) the various objects seem absorbed into the lavishly decorated textile onto which they are projected, and this despite the fact that the utensils and fruit are painted with extreme precision—whereas in Matisse's more systematic, colder works the objects are reduced to simple, scintillating signs. A more

INTERIOR WITH GOLDFISH, 1911. PUSHKIN MUSEUM OF FINE ART, MOSCOW.

perfect balance can be seen in *Still Life with a Geranium* (1910, Bayerische Staatsgemäldesammlung, Munich) where the composition is traversed by a broad strip of drapery, integrating a diversity of elements, including fragments of other pictures.

Matisse was now to develop this last-named practice to quite remarkable effect. Thus, for example, in the *Red Studio* (1911, Museum of Modern Art, New York), while ensuring the overall harmony of the composition by the use of the same rust-red hue for walls, floor and tablecloth, he scatters about it images of his own earlier paintings and sculptures, even of one of his ceramics. And the effect of these nuclei of vivid color is to give an amazing vitality to the picture surface. On several occasions Matisse "quoted" in his later works the *Dance*. A fragment of it, seen in foreshortening—and subjected, therefore, to some new distortions so as to reproduce its original rhythm—, combines with the tendrils of the plant in *Nasturtiums and the "Dance"*, to form an elegantly swaying arabesque. The large *Interior with Eggplants* (1911-1912, Grenoble Museum) is a *tour de force* of pictorial architectonics: the superposition on a single flat vertical plane, covering floor and wall, of a series of door-frames, windows, a screen, a buffet table with a vase on it —all reflected in a mirror on the left. Another "experiment with space" of this order takes place in the *Painter's Family* (1911, Hermitage, Leningrad), in which the figures bathed in uniform light that casts no shadows would seem devoid of any thickness —as if they were pinned to the picture surface—were it not that the long, black figure coming down to the bottom of the picture on the right and the angle at which the checkerboard is placed introduce a slanting rhythm into a composition otherwise rigorously frontal, while the geometrically patterned rug leads up, at the opposite corner, to the figure of a woman on a sofa, a wholly charming figure that might well have been the work of a sentimental "Nabi" painter.

PORTRAIT OF MADAME MATISSE, 1913. HERMITAGE, LENINGRAD.

THE MAJOR CADENCES

1911-1917

WHILE his art was thus taking its definitive form, gaining in scope and clarity, Matisse's private life was gradually settling down, in new surroundings, into its definitive rhythm. After a long noviciate, he had become, within a few years, the most conspicuous painter of the new generation; yet there were few who really understood him. And the more his reputation rose, the more Matisse, the man, withdrew himself, since at bottom he had little in common with most of his associates, and he had no disciples. Indeed his art followed a line of evolution whose bearing was known only to himself and a few initiates.

His venture into teaching, undertaken at the suggestion of Sarah Stein and the young German painter Hans Purrmann, one of his warmest admirers, tended, paradoxically enough, to increase his isolation. The "Académie Matisse" which functioned from 1908 to 1911, first in an expropriated convent, the Couvent des Oiseaux in the Rue de Sèvres, then in the former Couvent du Sacré-Cœur in the Boulevard des Invalides, was attended by over a hundred students, most of them Americans, Scandinavians and Germans, and few of whom, it must be admitted, were really capable of grasping his message. True, their numbers and enthusiasm testified to the prestige that Matisse was now beginning to enjoy abroad, but he, personally, was profoundly disappointed. For he soon discovered that his pupils merely wished to "learn the rules," and the deeper implications of his art, the freedom he sought to inculcate, were lost on them. As he wrote in his *Notes of a Painter* (1908), his view was that "rules have no existence outside of individuals."

We should bear in mind that, if his public dwindled at the very time when he was elevating his art towards a more generalized, more monumental form of expression, it was largely because his works did not always come into the hands of persons qualified to appreciate them. This has been the lot of most great painters in their early phase (Delacroix, fortunate in his patrons, was one of the rare exceptions). But Matisse was exceptionally unlucky, and this despite the fact that, from 1905 on, a few collectors, who soon became his friends, gave him generous support. Only one was French: the politician Marcel Sembat, who contributed an enthusiastic article to the *Cahiers d'Aujourd'hui* in 1913 and published the first monograph (1920) on the artist whose importance he had been amongst the first to recognize. Sembat built up a superb collection of Matisse's works, the finest of its kind in France, which he subsequently bequeathed to Grenoble Museum. However, less successful than Clemenceau in the case of Monet, he was unable to obtain official recognition for his protégé; it was not until 1925 that the Musée du Luxembourg, Paris, acquired a modest *Odalisque* by Matisse, though as far back as 1912 an outstanding still life had found its way to the Staatsgalerie of Munich, and in 1913 the National Museum of Stockholm had acquired Matisse's superb Moroccan landscape, *Park in Tangier*. Meanwhile the Steins were steadily adding to their collection of the key works and soon began to bring them to the notice of American collectors. But after 1906 most of Matisse's major works passed into the hands of that insatiable Russian Sergei Shchukin, who had already built up a fine collection of works of Cézanne, Gauguin, Renoir, Redon, the Douanier Rousseau and the Nabis. After the Revolution, Shchukin fled to France and, disheartened by the turn of events, seems to have lost interest in art. Meanwhile, however, he had acquired the greatest pictures painted by Matisse prior to 1914 and also no less than fifty paintings by Picasso, whom Matisse had generously introduced to him. For he had an equal admiration for both artists, and nothing of that sense of an antinomy between them which divided the Stein family, for example, into opposing camps. Other purchases of Matisse's works were made by Morosov, a Russian collector much younger than Shchukin, by some Germans and Scandinavians, and notably by Etta and Claribel Cone whose collection, presented to the Baltimore Museum of Art, is now world-famous.

Thus the bulk of Matisse's output from 1905 to 1914 was dispatched directly from his studio to collections in distant countries; only a few were exhibited in Paris (at the Salon d'Automne). Some privately owned works were loaned to exhibitions taking place abroad. Thus Shchukin arranged for showings of Matisse's work at the "Golden Fleece" salons of 1908 and 1909 in Moscow; the 1914 exhibition at the Gurlitt Gallery in Berlin contained nineteen pictures loaned by Michael Stein, and the exhibition organized by Walter Pach at the Montross Gallery, New York, in 1915, drew largely on American collections. But (to give a typical instance) the Moroccan paintings exhibited at Bernheim's in 1913 were promptly dispersed and not seen again for several decades. After the Russian Revolution Shchukin's and Morosov's collections were stored away and only reappeared much later, at the Museum of Modern Western Art in Moscow, then at the Hermitage in Leningrad and the Pushkin Museum in Moscow. Once they began to figure again in international exhibitions, for example the Brussels exhibition of 1958, it became clear that previous evaluations of Matisse's work as a whole needed to be drastically revised. And when we remember that in the United States some sixty works, several of them major ones, were housed by Dr Barnes in an educational Foundation accessible only to specialists, and that it is still forbidden to photograph them in color, we need not be surprised that for so long—notably in the period between the two World Wars—exhibitions of Matisse's art were restricted to his later output and no complete, objective estimate of his art as a whole was feasible. We owe it to the enlightened comprehension of the Soviet museums that we are able at long last to arrive at a balanced view of his life's work.

As a matter of fact Matisse found it relatively easy to reconcile himself to these conditions; he held that his works, once brought to fruition, could fend for themselves, no matter where they were. And, just as he had been glad to give up teaching, flattering as it might be to his self-esteem, he came to feel that all those heated controversies in which he once had shared, were so much "ancient history." More and more he tended to retire both from the agitations of the art world and from the tedious quest of public recognition. He let four years elapse between his first large one-man show—at Druet's in 1906—and the exhibition organized by Bernheim, who gave him a contract on very favorable terms. In 1913 he confined himself to exhibiting his latest Moroccan pictures and some sculpture, and thereafter made no attempt to catch the public eye, over a long period. Though occasionally he went abroad—for example to Berlin when Cassirer was arranging for his first exhibition in the German capital (Christmas, 1908), and to Moscow to visit Shchukin and see his collection (Matisse was disappointed by the way his pictures were hung)—he refrained from any steps that might give the impression he was taking part in publicizing his work in foreign lands. When he traveled it was solely to discover new sources of inspiration for his art and means of extending its scope. Thus in 1908 he visited Nuremberg with Purrmann to inspect the art treasures of that city and in 1910 went with Marquet to Munich for the Islamic Exhibition. What interested him most in Moscow were the icons he now saw for the first time. In the same spirit as when in 1898 he had "explored" Corsica and the South of France, he went in 1910 and 1911 to Spain and subsequently spent two winters in Tangier.

THE BLUE WINDOW, 1911. THE MUSEUM OF MODERN ART, NEW YORK,
MRS JOHN D. ROCKEFELLER, JR. PURCHASE FUND.

So as to be able to work in the tranquillity which had come to mean so much to him he moved, in 1909, to a country house, surrounded by trees and shrubberies, at Issy-les-Moulineaux (a few miles outside Paris). There was even a hothouse for the cultivation of the magnificent flowers in which Mme Matisse delighted. It was here that most of the large pictures of the following years were painted, until in January 1914 Matisse took to spending the winters at his old studio on the Quai Saint-Michel and working there as well. The big *Studios* and still lifes of 1911-1912 were painted at Issy, as were the first *Interiors with Goldfish* (Pushkin Museum of Fine Art, Moscow; Barnes Foundation, Merion; John Hay Whitney Collection, New York), the various works based on reminiscences of Andalusia and Tangier, the *Portrait of Mme Matisse in her Garden* (Hermitage, Leningrad), the *Windows* and views of the same garden and, finally, the realistic version of the *Music Lesson* (Barnes Foundation, Merion). In a trio of austerely grandiose compositions, painted in Paris, the *Interior with Goldfish* (1914, Baronne Gourgaud Collection, Paris), the *Studio, Quai Saint-Michel* (1916, Phillips Collection, Washington) and the *Painter and his Model* (Musée d'Art Moderne, Paris) we glimpse through the window on the right the geometrically ordered architecture of the Petit Pont and the Palais de Justice.

When we recall the paintings Matisse made at exactly the same spot in 1902, it is hard to believe that the setting is the same. What has changed here is the painter's vision and the setting has been conditioned by this, or, rather, has come to correspond to an idea that has gradually taken shape in the artist's mind. The formation of this idea was a joint effect of elements of very different origins, which had little by little coalesced. André Lhote's often quoted remark that Matisse proceeded from the sensation to the idea, unlike the Cubists who proceeded from the idea to the sensation, seems to me beside the mark. For example, Matisse's conception of the "glamour" of the Arab South *preceded* his Algerian trip, whose purpose was in fact to test out that conception. The *Blue Nude* of 1907, though sometimes subtitled "Souvenir de Biskra," is less a reminiscence of Matisse's visit to that town than a sort of composite tribute to the exotic fascinations of the Algerian scene. Then, when several years later he visited the exhibition of Islamic art in Munich, he found a "confirmation" (this was the word he used in conversation with Gaston Diehl) of what he had already sensed. The Persian miniatures revealed to him all that sensations can contain and signify beyond themselves. "By its accessories this art suggests a vaster space." But it was only after several years' rumination that he turned this discovery to practical account. This was when he took to spacing out isolated figures and objects on a black ground, like the decorative elements whose colors sing out, charged with an unwonted luster, against the opaque blackness of a vase or plate. Examples are the *Gourds* (Museum of Modern Art, New York) and the *Green Robe* (Private Collection, Paris).

That obsession with blue, so evident in Matisse's Moroccan landscapes, seems to have preceded his "discovery" of Tangier. We find a foretaste of it in that remarkable work the *Blue Window* (1911, Museum of Modern Art, New York), first element of a decorative ensemble planned for Paul Poiret, the famous couturier, who however found it too "advanced" and lost interest in the project. Here Matisse painted the view from his and his wife's bedroom at Issy with, in the foreground, toilet articles on a table; but all the details are highly synthesized and integrated into an all-over harmonic system, the forms of the trees outside the window being stylized into palms, and household articles transfigured into hieratic objects. The orderly vegetation of the Issy garden was soon to give place to the wild luxuriance of the Moroccan Gardens painted some months later, during Matisse's first stay at Tangier, the finest of which is in the National Museum, Stockholm. In these the delicate touches of mauve and the gentle twilight glow are reminiscent rather of the atmosphere of the Ile-de-France than of the brazen fervor of North African light. *Zorah Standing* (1911, Pushkin Museum, Moscow), where the young woman is posed against a reddish ground, the brown oval of the face spanned by large, wide-open eyes and the green robe trimmed with black-and-white braid, gives the impression of being much more schematized and stylized—an exotic replica of Holbein's *Christina of Denmark* —than is the charming likeness of the same model made the following year, *Zorah on the Terrace*, where the slim form of the young woman is set off by the triangle of pink sunlight on the left, the dark blue rug, the goldfish bowl and the embroidered slippers. The light effect is stronger and colors are intenser in *Window at Tangier* where the masses of leafage, buildings and small figures are no longer treated schematically but in well-marked, witty abbreviations in the manner of the views of Paris Matisse had painted years before in Marquet's company. In the *Entrance to the Kasbah*, on the other hand, where the figuration is far less precise, the effect is one of a delicate harmony of pale rose and various shades of blue. These three works, previously owned by Morosov, make an enchanting triptych in the reconstitution of his collection now on view in Leningrad.

Also in the two big figure compositions named *The Riffian* we find subtle variations on a given color scheme, whose dominant here is green. The Leningrad version, *Riffian Standing*, seems more on the surface, as a result of the flat planes of red and ochre of the face and arms standing out against the restless greens of the man's garment, and a delicately nuanced background.

WINDOW AT TANGIER, 1912. PUSHKIN MUSEUM OF FINE ART, MOSCOW.
(TEMPORARILY AT THE HERMITAGE, LENINGRAD)

ZORAH ON THE TERRACE, 1912. PUSHKIN MUSEUM OF FINE ART, MOSCOW
(TEMPORARILY AT THE HERMITAGE, LENINGRAD)

ENTRANCE TO THE KASBAH, 1912.
HERMITAGE, LENINGRAD.

80b

The three pictures, *Window at Tangier, Zorah on the Terrace* and *Entrance to the Kasbah*, sometimes called the "Moroccan Triptych," were painted by Matisse during his second stay at Tangier. All three were bought by the Russian collector Morosov, who hung them side by side, triptych-wise, in his apartment, *Zorah* being the central panel. Subsequently the three pictures were divided between the Pushkin Museum, Moscow, and the Hermitage at Leningrad. They have now been re-assembled in the last-named museum, and there is no question that they greatly gain by being presented as a triptych.

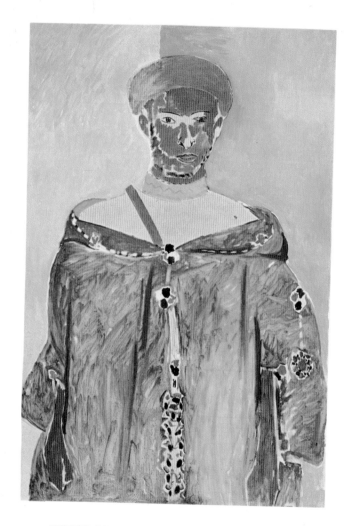

RIFFIAN STANDING, 1913. HERMITAGE, LENINGRAD.

The larger one in the Barnes Foundation is even more impressive, so powerful is the effect of the stalwart, splayed-out limbs planted on enormous feet, the expression of barbaric dignity on the face, divided by a tract of green shadow, the dark mass of the Arab cloak telling out against a curtain patterned with broad bands of blue and yellow and narrow streaks of green. In two other large works we find a synthesis of Matisse's responses to the Moroccan scene. The setting of the *Moorish Café* (Pushkin Museum of Fine Art, Moscow), with its row of arches, is frankly decorative, and the whole scene is bathed in a dim light from which emerge only the patches of ochre, oval or elongated, formed by faces or bare limbs. Painted in 1916 at Issy, after prolonged meditation on the treatment of the theme, the *Moroccans* (Museum of Modern Art, New York) goes still farther in the direction of symbolism and allusive form. The artist's memories have become stabilized and his previous ventures in this field consolidated. This is one of his most perfectly balanced compositions. Nothing could be more masterly than his arrangement of the picture elements reduced to pure symbols, self-complete signs set off by the jet-black ground. Thus flowers are represented as blue disks spanned by blue and white stripes, the mosque is suggested by a cupola and the figure in back view by the blue burnous and yellow turban.

Even when they embody new discoveries the Moroccan pictures have, by and large, a quite remarkable unity. In them breadth and simplicity, lyrical effusion and sobriety are admirably balanced. The free, fluent execution suggests that each was born in an enchanted moment, there was no need for preliminary sketches or for taking thought. Here Matisse has steered a prudent course between the perils of ornamental fantasy and decorative stylization—Scylla and Charybdis of the "orientalizing" artist—and achieved the dignity, austerity and freshness that characterize the greatest epochs of world art. It is evident that the North African scene was exceptionally propitious for the flowering of his genius; that here, *par excellence*, he achieved that "condensation of sensations" he speaks of in his *Notes of a Painter* as being essential to the work of art.

Nonetheless he was engaged at the same time—and there was nothing contradictory in this—in a series of intellectual, objective ventures which led him by gradual stages to the very frontier of abstraction. These are usually associated, if at a far remove, with the contemporary discoveries of the Cubists (who had now moved beyond the "analytic" phase), and even with those of the Futurists. Matisse, who had known Picasso since 1906, had studied Braque's early Cézannesque creations with interest, but he saw at once that this type of art was not for him; any fragmentation of the picture surface ran counter to all his natural inclinations. However, in the *Still Life with a Bust* (1912, Barnes Foundation, Merion) we find him trying out new procedures, and indicating space by the intersections of planes. Forms of objects are rendered by heavy outlines enclosing tracts of canvas untouched by the brush. But any effect of bleakness is remedied by a typically Matissian device, the insertion of a bunch of flowers rendered in pink and green touches with a yellow cluster in the center, painted directly on the neutral ground. Similarly he gives a personal, "human" imprint to the ascetically ordered *Woman on a High Stool* (1913-1914, Private Collection, Paris), whose abstract architectural schema he used as a referent in several later pictures. Also, the facial expression and posture of the seated woman reappear in some contemporary portraits—those of Yvonne Landsberg and Grete Prozor—but boldly simplified and condensed, and given a setting limited to a few "lines of construction" placed around the figure.

Even in 1909, while the broad rhythms of the *Dance* were beginning to preoccupy him, Matisse had been tempted to experiment with geometrical composition, as in *Conversation* (Pushkin

Museum, Moscow) where the bodies of two confronted figures are reduced to parallel verticals. But this was an exception; there could be no question of his abandoning these fluent curves, enclosing solids and forms in movement, which were fundamental to his art. In the *Portrait of Mme Matisse*, painted at Issy in 1913 (Hermitage, Leningrad), there is an exquisite grace in the flawless oval of the face, the perfect regularity of the features and the clear definition of the planes of color. In the *Portrait of Yvonne Landsberg*, however (1914, Philadelphia Museum of Art),

THE MOROCCANS, 1916. THE MUSEUM OF MODERN ART, NEW YORK, GIFT OF MR AND MRS SAMUEL A. MARX.

he rejects the blandishments of color and limits himself to a steel-grey, admirably suited for bringing out the complex play of lines distinctive of this portrait. The sculpturesque body is surrounded by an outcrop of white lines, generated by its forms and seeming to suggest its possible extensions in space, but this is done in a perfectly concrete manner—one is reminded of the wing-sheaths of some big insect. This picture (which much perturbed the sitter's family) now has an honored place in the Arensberg Collection (at the Philadelphia Museum of Art), alongside Marcel Duchamp's key works and the boldest creations of modern art. We find a similar system of sweeping curves organizing space in *Bathers by a River* (1916-1917, Henry Pearlman Collection, New York). But Matisse did not proceed further with the dissociation of figures into geometric forms, circles and ovals; no doubt he felt ill at ease in that rarefied atmosphere of the ultra-modern. Having demonstrated once again his versatility, he reverted—with happier results—to the architecturally ordered structure which came naturally to him.

In the *Piano Lesson* (Museum of Modern Art, New York) the organization of the picture surface by a combination of daring transpositions and more literal allusions, is an amazing *tour de force*. Demarcated by invisible lines, the big color planes are rigorously divided up by verticals and diagonals, onto which are grafted—like musical variations—graceful decorative arabesques, such as the iron window grill and the black woodwork of the music rack with the letters P.L.E.Y.E.L. showing in reverse. The basic grey tone, stressed by the blue and orange bands of the window and curtain, accentuates the bright pink of the piano top, while the green wedge (foliage in the garden) framed in the window and the converging lights playing on the small pianist's face amplify the sense of space. (On the grey background we see a sort of spectral emanation—or "negative"—of the *Woman on a High Stool*.) Though Matisse himself never

THE PIANO LESSON, 1916. THE MUSEUM OF MODERN ART, NEW YORK,
MRS SIMON GUGGENHEIM FUND.

made this clear, it would seem that the big *Music Lesson* (1917)
in the Barnes Foundation, in which the same theme is treated

THE STUDIO, QUAI SAINT-MICHEL, 1916. PHILLIPS COLLECTION, WASHINGTON.

realistically, was a second version, a more intimate, humanized interpretation of the subject. Here the artist has brought together all the members of his household in an agreeably domestic atmosphere, where the geometric substructure disappears under a wealth of vegetation and ornamental motifs. This picture illustrates the new orientation of Matisse's art, now that the high tension at which he had been working since 1913 was beginning to relax, and the urge to concentration and austerity of the early war years was wearing off.

Already the large *Studios* of 1916 had pointed to the change that now was coming over his outlook. The same impulse that had led to the exaltation of characteristic forms in the *Gourds* now led him to depict each figure—reclining nude, seated model or the painter at his easel—as a self-sufficient entity rendered by a single dominant color or a simple color chord, and defined by a single contour line. Nonetheless Matisse linked up individual forms between themselves by means of the architectural layout, without impairing the intensity they acquired as isolated units. And he achieved an equal monumentality when he centered the composition on quite ordinary objects glorified by this intensive scrutiny—as in those masterpieces of inspired simplicity, the *Pewter Jug* (Cone Collection, Baltimore Museum of Art), the *Lemon* (Barnes Foundation, Merion), the *Lorrain Chair* (Private Collection, Solothurn). Here once again the characteristic decorative arabesque makes its appearance in the backdrop; the fruit and glass of water tell out against the whiteness of the scallop-edged dish (in the *Pewter Jug*), while black resumes its role of a support for the cool tints.

Thus we see Matisse at his best not in his "extremist" works but in the serenely balanced ones. He displays a well-nigh infallible sense of the exact limits he must set himself if he is to achieve perfection in each successive work. Hence his gift of holding his breath, so to speak, and curbing his immediate

impulses. Yet, when it is a matter of discovering the right tone, he does not care if he seems to be reverting to the past; and, despite a strict control of his means, he always bends his will to his natural inclinations. Had not Apollinaire, as far back as 1907, in his first study of Matisse, spoken of "an order of which instinct sets the measure"?

THE PEWTER JUG, 1916-1917. BALTIMORE MUSEUM OF ART, CONE COLLECTION.

INTERIOR WITH A VIOLIN, 1917-1918.
STATENS MUSEUM FOR KUNST, COPENHAGEN.

THE LUXURY OF CALM
1917-1954

Now that the major works of the years 1905-1912 had gone abroad and the experimental works of recent years had been completed and laid by in the studio (they were not exhibited until 1927, at Paul Guillaume's), Matisse could, at last, allow himself a breathing space. Indeed he may well have felt fatigued after so many efforts to strike out in new directions. Or was it that he feared there was too wide a gulf between what the public, no longer hostile, expected of him and the heights, ever harder of access and bare of all concessions, that he aspired to scale? I do not think he now refused to hear the "call of the absolute" or had any thought of abandoning the quest, but he may well have seen a risk of ceasing to master the forces he had unleashed. In any case the program he had originally set himself gave ample scope for his creative energies, and he now set to realizing it in depth. For since the declaration of faith published in the *Grande Revue*, his ideal had never changed; he still dreamt of "an art of balance, purity and serenity, devoid of troubling or obsessive subject matter" that would act as "an appeasing influence, a mental sedative, rather like a good armchair."

Perhaps, too, after so much exacting studio work he felt a need to get away from Paris and steep himself once more in nature and sunlight. In 1917 he again joined forces with Marquet whom he always looked on as his exemplar in the investigation of "real life" and direct observation of the motif. In the summer he visited Marquet at Chenonceaux, and in the following winter moved to Marseilles where his friend had rented a room in the home of the writer Eugène Monfort (to this period date Marquet's fine sketches of figures in the street viewed in fore-shortening from his window). Then Matisse caught bronchitis and had to move to a milder climate; this he found at Nice, where he took a room at the Hôtel Beau-Rivage. Nice spelt the beginning of a new chapter in his life, for it was there that he encountered the mellow light which was to bathe the art of his subsequent career; it was to Nice, as to a home port, that he regularly returned year after year, and it was in Nice that he was to find his last resting place. "When I realized that morning after morning I'd see that light, I could hardly believe my luck!" so he told Georges Salles, who quoted the remark in his fore-word to the 1950 exhibition at Nice, and all Matisse's work, up to his death, reflects this sunlit joy.

The simple hotel bedroom, from which through the slats of the Venetian blinds he had glimpses of the sea, and whose curtains rippled daylong in the Mediterranean breeze, provided Matisse with the "escape" of which he had so long been dream-ing; with freedom to combine, as the fancy took him, the most unlikely elements, and, last but not least, with a "neutral" atmosphere that liberated him from the too familiar décor of a well-appointed home. In the limited space between toilet table and bed he managed to find room for his easel, and in this simple setting he has depicted himself engaged in painting (*Self-Portrait*, Private Collection), absorbed in his work and at peace with the world. In the *Interior with a Violin* (Copenhagen) he has placed in front of the window the violin on which, like Ingres, he daily played—another discipline of evasion. Here the glowing color of the wood vibrates in a pool of shadows that at once brings out and harmonizes the blue, red and yellow of violin case, table cover and chair. (This perfectly balanced work was one of Matisse's favorites.) Meanwhile he kept to the expressive, never inert, areas of black of his previous period, presenting them either in masses as in the *Black Table* (Hahnloser Collection, Bern), or in bands stressing the foreground, as in the "Windows" which so much impressed Renoir.

George Besson, who was present on these occasions, has described Matisse's visits to Renoir at Cagnes, the friendship that quickly sprang up between them, and also Matisse's meetings with Bonnard at Antibes. Though the three men stood for generations very different in taste and outlook, they shared the same ideal, that of creating a world of serene, smiling beauty. Sometimes Matisse worked in the open, on the hills above Nice, Montboron and Montalban, making small landscapes that he completed in two or three sessions. But short-sighted as he was, he found the glare too strong, and preferred interior scenes where the light, filtered through Venetian blinds, flooded all objects with a gentle radiance. Gradually he took to the use of opalescent colors—delicate harmonies of pale pink, bluish grey and limpid green—having the fluidity of watercolor.

When in 1918, on his return to Nice after a short stay in Paris, he found that the Beau-Rivage had been requisitioned, Matisse moved to the nearby Hôtel de la Méditerranée where he had a larger and better bedroom. The lofty French window, giving on a balcony, the floral wallpaper, white moldings, toilet table and the upholstered chair provided for the model figure in several compositions (e.g. *French Window at Nice*, Barnes Foundation, and *Interior at Nice*, Mrs Gilbert Chapman Collection, New York). Matisse was fond of having pretty young women pose in Moorish costumes and turbanlike headdresses, usually rendering little more than their general effect; sometimes, however, he lingered over an exceptionally interesting face, that for instance of "Antoinette" which, at first treated a little heavily and tentatively, is seen to perfection, with its ebony black tresses and the fantastic hat made by the painter himself, in *White Plumes* (Göteborg and Minneapolis; also several drawings).

In 1921 he decided to settle down in Nice for good, while keeping a residence in Paris, and his choice fell on an apartment in the Old Town, with a view of the Mediterranean over the low roofs of Les Ponchettes. He fitted out a corner of his studio in oriental style, with a superb, richly decorated Moorish screen, Arab rugs, and curtains—an exotic setting oddly out of keeping with such figures as the boys in striped blazers in the *Checker Game* (Private Collection, Paris), the girl in the pastel *Piano Lesson* (Ryan Middleton Collection, Dundee) or the chic young women in *The Moorish Screen* (Philadelphia Museum). In each instance Matisse re-adjusts these over-insistent decorative elements so as both to give them more flexibility and to reduce them to patterns of stripes or colored checkerwork, creating in the heart of the composition a zone of warmth and gaiety, within which figures (posed in telling attitudes), bunches of flowers, vases and other objects fall elegantly into place. Though he has a fondness for compositions centering on graceful human figures, he sometimes contents himself, during this period, with arrangements of fruit and flowers having a vibrant vitality of their own, compositions to which the French term for a still life, *nature morte*, seems singularly inappropriate.

Though none can deny the exquisite charm of these frail young women dressed in exotic costumes, cloistered behind Venetian blinds or half-drawn curtains, dreaming the hours away in a gentle languor, many have deplored the great number of "odalisques" painted by Matisse in the period 1920-1925, the implication being that he could not help repeating himself and in the end becoming tedious. Yet when we examine with care this—admittedly long—series of figure compositions, we cannot fail to be struck by the painter's unvarying success, the way in which, in every instance, he has singled out the "happy moment." They compose harmonious suites of subtle variations on a few given themes, and a selection of the most characteristic examples of each would show the artist advancing, year by year, from strength to strength. First, then, we have the elongated, beautifully modeled figure in *Meditation (Après le Bain*, 1920,

INTERIOR AT NICE, 1921.
COLLECTION MRS GILBERT CHAPMAN, NEW YORK.

APRÈS LE BAIN (MEDITATION), 1920.
COLLECTION MRS ALBERT D. LASKER, NEW YORK.

THE HINDU POSE, 1923.
COLLECTION DONALD STRALEM, NEW YORK.

Mrs Albert D. Lasker Collection, New York); next the *Seated Moorish Woman* (1922, Barnes Foundation); then the *Odalisque with Raised Arms* (1923, Art Institute of Chicago), and finally the *Hindu Pose* (1923, Donald Stralem Collection, New York). In all these works the vigorous construction makes its full effect, without detriment to the color magic of the whole. This was, too, the time when Matisse took to using an exceptionally flexible design enveloping both model and setting in the same arabesque—whereas his lithographs of the period were still of a frankly descriptive order.

He also made a great many small pictures, having the size and look of *pochades*, since he always stopped short once he had reached the climactic point of each, devised a novel harmony, and recorded the exact form that had impressed itself on his vision. In these, sensation was rendered in its purest state and it would have been useless, not to say injurious, to try to go farther. The dimensions of these works are no criterion of their relative importance, since Matisse always made a point of adapting his composition to the surface to be covered. A perfect balance between these two factors was his prime concern, and this is delightfully evident in almost all these small works; hence it is not surprising that they were so eagerly snapped up by connoisseurs at the annual exhibitions in the Bernheim-Jeune gallery. Many have found their way to the Barnes Foundation and the Cone Collection, and most of them are little masterpieces of their kind. Meanwhile, however, Matisse was investigating new types of subject, though he did not linger long over any. Thus, during his summer stays at Etretat in 1920 and 1921 (the notion of spending the summer months on the Riviera was, in those days, unthinkable), he took to painting the familiar sights of the seashore: seaweed, shellfish, conger eels, rays and fish of various species, with their colors fading on the sand as the catch was unloaded by the fishermen. Henceforth these marine forms were to be incorporated in his magic universe. He also made a number of landscapes, slightly abridged in the manner of Marquet; for example the *Cliff*, pitted with holes and fringed with pink in the Cone Collection, and a view of boats drawn up on the beach seen in the black frame of an open window (Dauberville Collection, Paris).

The period following the First World War divided contemporary artists into two camps; there seemed to be no mid-course between the irrational outbursts and extravagances of the wave of Expressionism that was sweeping Europe and the reactionary, rather arid art, claiming "Latin" inspiration, that went by the name of Neo-Classicism. Under these conditions Matisse's retirement from the mêlée was an act of the highest wisdom, and it was remarkably fruitful in results. Avoiding both extremes and all temptations to revert to the formulas of an atrophied tradition, Matisse, like some medieval alchemist, wrought out an art of strange enchantments, an antidote for the malaise of a troubled age.

From 1925 onwards we find him moving towards a mode of expression in which, while intensifying his colors, he succeeded in retaining both the subtlety and the boldness of his chromatic harmonies. Similarly his figures, while still keeping to their decorative role, became more monumental. Facilitated perhaps by his practice of thinking out each step beforehand, this evolution is plain to see in such works as *Odalisque with a Tambourine* (1926, Mr and Mrs William S. Paley Collection, New York) and *Ballet Dancer* (1927, Cone Collection, Baltimore Museum), where the figures undergo a curious displacement, interpreting by means of planes of color the changes due to the play of shadows and perspective recession. In *Woman with a Veil* (1927, Mr and Mrs William S. Paley Collection, New York) we find some of the idioms of the 1915-1916 portraits of the model Lorette, the shaded portions of the figure merging into the dark hues of the background. *Decorative Figure on an Ornamental Background* (1927, Musée d'Art Moderne, Paris)—whose very title is revealing—and the 1928 series of Odalisques, *Seated Odalisque* (Cone Collection, Baltimore Museum), *Reclining Odalisque* (Petit Palais, Paris) and *Two Odalisques playing Checkers* (Ralph F. Colin Collection, New York; National Museum, Stockholm) are, *inter alia*, miracles of structural organization.

TWO ODALISQUES PLAYING CHECKERS, 1928.
COLLECTION RALPH F. COLIN, NEW YORK.

DECORATIVE FIGURE ON AN ORNAMENTAL BACKGROUND, 1927.
MUSÉE D'ART MODERNE, PARIS.

THE PINK NUDE, 1935. BALTIMORE MUSEUM OF ART, CONE COLLECTION.

to any shape and moved back and forth until he lit on a fully satisfying arrangement. But when the mural was set in place at Merion, it turned out that the measurements originally given were incorrect, notably that the soffits of the pendentives were twice as wide as had been calculated. Nothing daunted, Matisse started all over again and, after many preliminary designs, produced a second version differing considerably from the first. There are more figures, each lunette contains a pair of dancers,

THE DREAM, 1940. PRIVATE COLLECTION, PARIS.

and a seated figure occupies the springing of each soffit. In the first version the dancing women were directly linked together. In the second more emphasis is laid on the static elements of the composition, though the figures are more aerial and their upward, soaring movement is accentuated, a movement implemented by the vertical arrangement of the blue, pink and black bands of the background. But the first version, more hieratic in character and complete in itself independently of the architectural context, is in no way inferior to the second. It was acquired by the City of Paris, thanks to the efforts of Raymond Escholier, seconded by Gabriel Hanotaux and Louis Gillet. Unfortunately, however, this masterpiece, the envy of so many great art museums, has never been hung and lies, rolled up, in the cellars of the Petit-Palais. Only once has it been exhibited; at the Exhibition of Mural Art given in 1948 in the Palais des Papes at Avignon. Hung, under Matisse's instructions, on high supports, at a slightly sloping angle below the vaulting of the chapel, the three panels produced an unforgettable impression on all who were privileged to see them.

While a series of Matisse retrospectives was taking place —at the Georges Petit Gallery in Paris, at the Kunsthalle, Basel, and at the recently founded Museum of Modern Art, New York (followed up by exhibitions in many other parts of the world, including Tokyo in 1951)—Matisse was entering on yet another experimental phase, which was to last almost until his death. "Experimental" is perhaps inappropriate; such was his mastery that each successive work seemed born full-fledged, inevitable. He took to employing a great diversity of techniques, freeing himself from the restraints they normally impose and approaching compositional problems from a quite new angle. While engaged on the monumental task of the Merion murals, he was also working on the illustrations (29 etchings) of the *Poems of Mallarmé*, commissioned by Albert Skira. This was his first, and supreme, achievement in a form of art that he was destined to transfigure. At the beginning of the century Bonnard had created a masterpiece, at once traditional and spontaneous, in his illustrations of Verlaine's *Parallèlement*. In his very first venture in this field Matisse imposed a modern style on the art of illustration, which now became a self-sufficient "plastic equivalent" of the text, playing an autonomous, vital part in the

WOMAN WITH ETRUSCAN VASE, 1940. THE CLEVELAND MUSEUM OF ART.

structure of the book. The etcher's needle gives an incomparable clarity to Matisse's line; all these forms, even the wealth of hair in *La chevelure* and the rippling plumage in *Le cygne*, seem like so many facets of an exquisitely cut diamond. Nowhere else have his observations on drawing as "generating light" and providing the purest source of emotion been so fully justified.

PINEAPPLE AND ANEMONES, 1940.
COLLECTION MRS ALBERT D. LASKER, NEW YORK.

LEMONS AND SAXIFRAGE, 1943. S. ROSENGART COLLECTION, LUCERNE.

In his subsequent book illustrations, however, Matisse usually employed the lithographic crayon which gave a fuller sweep to the arabesque and whose line could be thickened or thinned at will. And he imparted to this often rather blurred technique a wholly personal accent, combining forthright vigor with the tenderest sensibility.

After so successfully coping with the problems set by large-scale murals, Matisse found the limitations of the easel picture somewhat irksome. However, after an interval of some years, he developed the methods tentatively employed in 1916 and returned to the presentment of surfaces illuminated by chords of color, soon stepped up to a remarkable intensity. The advance made from the *Magnolia Branch* (1934, Cone Collection), with its leafage faintly quivering amid a pattern of lightly indicated decorative motifs, to the *Pink Nude* (in the same collection) is revealing. Its special interest lies in the way in which the artist went about the creation of the latter work, as recorded in photographs of its twenty-two successive states between May 3 and October 30, 1935. To begin with, we have a very ordinary couch whose dense blue surface is organized first in vertical stripes, then in a plaid pattern; next, we see the forms gradually expanding, bound by a melodious contour line, the head abandoning the (natural) languorous pose and straightening up, and the decorative elements of the vase of flowers and chair combining into a single, composite ornamental motif.

In the same year Matisse made a tapestry cartoon, *Window at Tahiti* (Le Cateau Museum), for Mme Cuttoli; in this a boat he had sketched from his balcony at Papeete is presented in a lavishly ornamented setting. In 1938 he was commissioned by Nelson A. Rockefeller to paint an overmantel for his apartment; this contains four large figures, the two below in static poses, those above disposed in flowing, brightly colored arabesques. These two girls reappear in *Music* (1939, Albright Art Gallery, Buffalo). Photographs of successive stages of the work in progress show the composition "growing like a plant," thickening in its upper part, with the guitar player seemingly hung in air in a broadly rendered mass of foliage. Matisse had fitted up a large studio in his new residence at Cimiez and here, until 1941, he produced a series of figures posed against settings of leafage (e.g. the *Woman with Etruscan Vase*, Cleveland Museum), and also of more strongly individualized faces, sometimes treated as living allegories, as in *La France* and

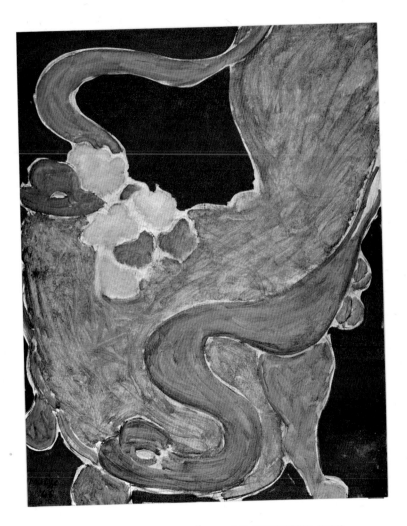

THE ROCAILLE CHAIR, 1946. PRIVATE COLLECTION, PARIS.

The Dream (Private Collection, Paris) and *The Rumanian Blouse* (Musée d'Art Moderne, Paris); as well as numerous still lifes such as *Oysters* (Basel), *Pineapple and Anemones* (Mrs Albert D. Lasker Collection, New York) and *Magnolia* (Musée d'Art Moderne, Paris). Many who called on him at Cimiez in those years have spoken of Matisse's huge aviary filled with exotic birds, the cooing of turtledoves that greeted the visitor in the living room, and described the studio cluttered up with homely or exotic objects, the "fetishes" glorified by Matisse in his paintings: rare vases, Negro masks, Chinese pottery, seashells, lemons, dry gourds and hothouse plants.

When this spate of production was cut short by a very serious operation (in Lyons), Matisse, now compelled to work lying down, reverted to drawing and book illustration, first at Cimiez, then at Vence, where he took a villa called Le Rêve. It was here that, having difficulty in manipulating his paints, he took to using painted paper, cut into the desired shapes. Hence that extraordinary portfolio of "chromatic and rhythmic improvisations," named *Jazz*, in which a crystallization of his memories of the circus, folk tales and travels is embodied in vivid, eye-filling images. So as both to link them together and to modulate their contrasts, Matisse added a commentary written in a large flowing hand, which contains some striking aphorisms, such as "Cutting to the quick in color reminds me of direct cutting in sculpture" and "My curves do not run wild."

Nothing could be more remarkable than the way in which, by dint of perseverance and careful planning, Matisse managed to overcome the disabilities of an enfeebled constitution, and continued working as hard as ever. Indeed he found that by shepherding his energies he still could undertake and carry out large-scale projects. In 1946, using the same cut-and-pasted paper technique as in *Jazz*, he made cartoons for two companion tapestries, *Polynesia, the Sky* and *Polynesia, the Sea*, which were

PLUM BLOSSOMS, GREEN BACKGROUND, 1948.
COLLECTION MRS ALBERT D. LASKER, NEW YORK.

SMALL BLUE INTERIOR, 1947. PRIVATE COLLECTION, PARIS.

woven by the National Tapestry Factory at Beauvais; also for two decorative linen wall hangings for Ascher and Co. based on Oceanian motifs. Then a fairly long respite from his malady enabled him to take up his brush again. In this last, grandiose series of paintings (1946-1948) we find a steady advance, proceeding from studies of rhythmic form at its purest (*Rocaille Chair*, Private Collection, Paris), of balance (*Small Blue Interior*, Private Collection, Paris) or of organization ("Still Lifes with Pomegranates"), up to the large compositions of 1948: *The Egyptian Curtain* (Phillips Collection, Washington), the *Pineapple* (Private Collection, New York), *Plum Blossoms, Green Background* (Mrs Albert D. Lasker Collection, New York), *Plum Blossoms, Ochre Background*, the *Black Fern* and, crowning all, the *Large Interior in Red* (Musée d'Art Moderne, Paris). The complete ease of the execution, the total absence of any hesitations or pentimenti, are products of an art so perfectly accomplished that it brings forth rare, unlooked-for beauties without the slightest trace of effort.

The great Matisse exhibition which took place at the Musée d'Art Moderne, Paris, in 1949 was remarkable for its revelation of the many new avenues the artist was opening up. Matisse himself devoted especial care to it—something which he had been unable to do for many years, but which, to his thinking, was called for on this occasion. For what the eighty-year-old artist aimed at was not to give a résumé of a long life's work, but to open prospects on the future. He showed the whole series of the last two years' paintings, the tapestries and linen panels and the books he had recently illustrated: *Jazz*, the *Love Letters of a Portuguese Nun, Les Fleurs du Mal*, the Anthology of Ronsard's *Amours*, the *Poèmes de Charles d'Orléans* and André Rouveyre's *Repli*. To these he added his first compositions in *papiers découpés* (still of small dimensions) and a magnificent suite of twenty-two brush drawings in Indian ink made at the same time as the 1947 and 1948 paintings. All these works, on more or less analogous themes, convey by a variety of means a vision of an ideal world of blissful ease. Lingering memories of the South Seas and far-off lands are evident in tranquil renderings of luxurious vegetation, swaying palms, gorgeous fruits and flowers, dahlias, pineapples, pomegranates. Relatively small as are their formats, these pictures open vistas on unknown dimensions and carry novel resonances. And similarly the books with lithographic illustrations, always constructed with an eye to the perfectly balanced presentment of all their elements, give the effect of symphonic poems by a great composer. In the Indian ink compositions, intense blacks blossom out into forms suggesting all the nuances of color, while the motifs cut from paper colored with gouache closely follow the contour of each image and the palpitations of the line.

In the Chapel at Vence the floor in white marble slabs with small black lozenges reflects the ever-changing gleams of colored light (inspired, one would say, by the cut-and-pasted papers) streaming in from the stained-glass windows. From 1948 on Matisse concentrated all his energy on the Chapel, planning out both the exterior and interior architecture and the entire decor-ation. Raymond Escholier has told us that the first notion of this chapel came to Matisse while he was lying ill in the Clinique du Parc at Lyons, where a young Dominican nun, Sister Marie-Ange, tended him with devoted care. Just opposite Matisse's villa at Vence was a conventual rest home for invalid girls, belonging to the same religious Order. On his return he was looked after by a nurse serving in the home, Sister Marie-Jacques, a refugee from La Vendée, who consented to pose for drawings (it is believed that she was the model for the "Portu-guese Nun"). When she became a Dominican novice Matisse decided to go through with the project he had formed when ill at Lyons of carrying out an enterprise of this kind. Here there was no question of installing works by the best modern artists in an already existing church, as had been done at Assy. Matisse's aim was to create an atmosphere appropriate to the spirit of the Dominican Order in an entirely new edifice and thus to ensure total homogeneity between the building and its decorations. On a ground of white glazed tiles stand out three major motifs: a huge *St Dominic* reduced to the flawless oval of the face and the long folds of the cloak; a flowerlike *Virgin and Child* surrounded by stylized flowers; and a *Stations of the Cross* composed of elementary signs like those of the Catacombs but, unlike them, in full light. This austere Dominican tone-poem in black and white, in which the only "colorful" details are the richly worked door of the Confessional and liturgical accessories, is illuminated, differently according to the hour of the day, by green and yellow stained-glass windows, and (according to Matisse) the best time to visit the Chapel is the end of a winter morning when the light is at its purest. No visitor, believer or otherwise, can fail to have a feeling, on entering, that he is participating in a spiritual communion of the noblest order. "I want those who enter my chapel," Matisse told Father Couturier, "to feel purified and delivered of their burdens." And in 1952 he concluded his message to his birthplace with the words: "It was in making the Vence chapel that I truly 'found myself' and I realized that my long life's labors had been directed to the service of the great human family, which needed to be given glimpses of the unfading beauty of the world, through my intermediary." This labor of love was continued and completed just before his death by the big horizontal stained-glass window presented to the Le Cateau Infant School and placed at ground level in the playroom of the smallest children, whose drawings, I noticed, often reflect something of its color magic.

Matisse's whole life was dedicated to the service of beauty and he kept faith with it to the very end. Between 1950 and 1954,

CHINESE FISHES, 1951. CUT-AND-PASTED PAPER. PRIVATE COLLECTION, PARIS.

ZULMA, 1950. CUT-AND-PASTED PAPER.
STATENS MUSEUM FOR KUNST, COPENHAGEN.

with his *papiers découpés* colored with flat gouaches, he added a whole new chapter to his œuvre. It was not because he could no longer hold his brushes—the 1948 paintings prove the contrary—that Matisse explored the utmost possibilities of the new technique he had invented, radically different both from cubist *papiers collés* and from surrealist *collages*. Nor was it a matter of combining "pre-fabricated" forms and exploiting their chance encounters, but of capturing and defining forms instinct with life and movement, and presenting color in dense, glowing masses. Matisse wished the most characteristic of these compositions, the large nude *Zulma* (1950, Copenhagen) and *Sadness of the King* (1952, Musée d'Art Moderne, Paris), to figure in the Salon de Mai alongside the works of young contemporary artists. But most of the works in this technique remained in the form of the strips of colored paper arranged by the artist on the walls, ceiling and floor of his apartment. Thanks to the precise instructions he had left, his helper, Lydia Delektorskaya, was able to assemble them on canvas or on panels and they were shown to the public in 1959, first in a special issue of *Verve*, then in an exhibition at the Kunsthalle, Bern.

In the 1950 and 1951 panels Matisse grouped isolated signs, both concrete and synthetic, inspired by marine fauna and flowers: *Creatures of the Sea, Chinese Fishes, Snowflowers*. The various motifs were presented on squares placed side by side, in the manner of glazed tiles. To that prolific year 1952 date the large-scale compositions: *Sadness of the King* and *The Negress*. In the latter Matisse has imparted a peculiar intensity to passages of red and black gouache spaced out in isolated forms, but animated with so natural a movement that they suffice to people an entire wall. In the *Blue Nudes*, on the other hand, the masses of the bodies, rendered in monochrome, are separated only by a thin white line (one of the painter's oldest procedures) and the surface is completely filled by them. There are several sequences of these nudes, some shown in movement, e.g. *Women Dancing*, others in static, compact geometric forms; others, again, treated in a sort of shorthand, blend into the overall arabesque, e.g. the slim forms of his "Rope Dancers." In the case of one of these, Matisse, as he had no more blue paper

ACANTHI, 1954. CUT-AND-PASTED PAPER. PRIVATE COLLECTION, PARIS.

handy, completed the legs with paper of another color and in this composition, known as *The Green Stockings*, we have what in the past was one of his favorite color combinations. Lastly, in the big horizontal panels, "Swimming Pools," we see, disposed on lengths of natural-colored canvas, men and women diving, floating on their backs, or cutting capers, sometimes leaping beyond the frame, like dolphins skimming the waves.

In 1953 we find Matisse reverting to the style of his drawings of 1947-1948; line does more to implement the color, whether helping to define its outlines or combining with it broad streaks of Indian ink. In the *Acrobats* the distortions of bodies tensed by muscular strain are conveyed by the cutting of the painted paper, strips of which dilate or contract almost as if endowed with life. In other works bodies drawn with the brush alternate with decorative patches of color. We find this in the huge polyptych named *Grande Décoration aux Masques*; measuring ten yards by three and a half, it reveals the artist's creative energy and inventiveness at their splendid best, in the constant variations of the symmetrical, yet never identical, forms of leaves, petals and pistils of flowers. The composition of *The Snail* is wholly chromatic: a pattern of rectangles of unequal sizes and different colors caught up in a slow spiral movement. And then at the close of his life, Matisse conjured up, for the last time, memories of the "earthly paradise" of the South Seas, and produced compositions on purely floral motifs, having the freshness and the subtle fragrance of the Song of Songs: *Vine, Ivy* and *Poppies* all in graceful arabesques, and the *Acanthi*, green, yellow, red and orange tongues of fire darting like arrows into the vastness of ambient space.

Such was the enchanting simplicity of Matisse's last terrestrial vision, his swan song, finale of the vast œuvre built up through the years—a treasure house as rich in strange and delicate delights as any fabled palace of the East.

SELECTED BIBLIOGRAPHY

A detailed bibliography up to 1951, compiled by Bernard KARPEL, was published in Alfred H. BARR, Jr., *Matisse, His Art and His Public*, Museum of Modern Art, New York 1951. For the period 1951-1966, see the bibliography in the catalogue of the Henri Matisse Retrospective, University of California at Los Angeles, 1966; for the period 1966-1970, see the catalogue of "Henri Matisse, Exposition du Centenaire," Grand Palais, Paris 1970.

Monographs

M. SEMBAT, *Matisse et son œuvre*, Nouvelle Revue Française, Paris 1920.
— C. VILDRAC, *Cinquante dessins de Henri Matisse* (preface), Paris 1920.—
R. SCHACHT, *Henri Matisse*, Dresden 1922. — A. BASLER, *Henri Matisse*,
Leipzig 1924. — W. GEORGE, *Dessins de Henri Matisse*, Quatre Chemins,
Paris 1925. — F. FELS, *Henri Matisse*, Chroniques du Jour, Paris 1929. —
A. BERTRAM, *Henri Matisse*, Studio, London, and Rudge, New York 1930.
— R. FRY, *Henri Matisse*, E. Weyhe, New York 1930. — G. JEDLICKA,
Henri Matisse, Chroniques du Jour (in German), Paris 1930. — A. C.
BARNES and C. DE MAZIA, *The Art of Henri Matisse*, Scribner's, New York
1933. — P. COURTHION, *Henri Matisse*, Rieder, Paris 1934. — R. KAWA-
SHIMA, *Matisse*, Tokyo 1936. — R. ESCHOLIER, *Henri Matisse*, Floury,
Paris 1937.—A. ROMM, *Henri Matisse*, Leningrad 1937.—C. ROGER-MARX,
Dessins de Henri Matisse, Braun, Paris 1939. — J. CASSOU, *Matisse*, Couleur
des Maîtres, Braun, Paris 1939; English translation, Tudor, New York
1939. — P. COURTHION, *Le Visage de Matisse*, Marguerat, Lausanne 1943.
— G. BESSON, *Matisse*, Braun, Paris 1943. — L. ARAGON, *Matisse en France*,
in *Matisse: Dessins, Thèmes et Variations*, Fabiani, Paris 1943. — I. GRÜNE-
WALD, *Matisse och expressionismen*, Wahlström & Widstrand, Stockholm
1944. — L. SWANE, *Henri Matisse*, Norstedts, Stockholm 1944. — M.
VALSECCHI, *Disegni di Henri Matisse*, Hoepli, Milan 1944. — L. ARAGON,
Matisse, Skira, Geneva 1946. — G. SCHEIWILLER, *Henri Matisse*, Hoepli,
Milan 1947. — A. ROMM, *Matisse, A Social Critique*, Lear, New York 1947.
— A. LEJARD, *Matisse*, Hazan, Paris 1948. — M. MALINGUE, *Matisse,
Dessins*, Éditions des Deux Mondes, Paris 1949. — A. H. BARR Jr.,
Matisse, His Art and his Public, Museum of Modern Art, New York 1951.
— G. DIEHL, *Henri Matisse*, Fernand Nathan, Paris 1952. — A. VERDET,
Prestiges de Matisse, Emile Paul, Paris 1952. — C. GREENBERG, *Henri
Matisse*, Abrams, New York 1953. — G. DIEHL, *Henri Matisse*, Tisné,
Paris 1954; English translation, Paris 1958. — G. BESSON, *Henri Matisse*,
Braun, Paris 1954. — G. JEDLICKA, *Die Matisse-Kapelle in Vence*, Frankfort
1955. — W. S. LIEBERMAN, *Etchings by Matisse*, Museum of Modern Art,
New York 1955. — R. ESCHOLIER, *Matisse ce vivant*, Fayard, Paris 1956.

In addition to dictionaries and histories of modern art, the following may also be consulted:

H. MALPEL, *Notes sur l'art d'aujourd'hui et peut-être de demain*, Paris 1911. — A. SOFFICI, *Trois post-impressionnistes, Gauguin, Matisse, Seurat* in *Le Néo-classicisme dans l'art contemporain*, Rome 1923. — M. RAYNAL, *Anthologie de la peinture en France de 1906 à nos jours*, Paris 1927. — G. STEIN, *Autobiography of Alice B. Toklas*, London & New York 1933. — C. ZERVOS, *Histoire de l'art contemporain*, Paris 1938. — P. MAROIS, *Des goûts et des couleurs*, Albin Michel, Paris 1947. — G. DUTHUIT, *Les Fauves*, Trois Collines, Geneva 1949; English translation, *The Fauvist Painters*, Wittenborn-Schultz, New York 1950. — M. G. MICHEL, *De Renoir à Picasso*, Fayard, Paris 1955.

Special Issues of Magazines

E. FAURE, J. ROMAINS, C. VILDRAC and L. WERTH, *Les Cahiers d'Aujourd'hui*, Crès, Paris 1921; new revised edition, 1923. — P. FIERENS, P. GUÉGUEN, G. SALLES, R. FRY, H. McBRIDE, W. GROHMANN, K. ASPLUND, G. SCHEIWILLER, G. APOLLINAIRE, C. ZERVOS, *Cahiers d'Art*, No. 5-6, Paris 1931; English version, E. Weyhe, New York 1931. — *Pour et contre Matisse*, special number of *Les Chroniques du Jour*, articles by A. LHOTE, R. REY, W. GEORGE, G. ROUAULT, F. FELS, A. LEVINSON, R. FRY, F. NEUGASS, P. FIERENS, C. ROGER-MARX, G. APOLLINAIRE, L. VAUXCELLES, C. ZERVOS, M. SEMBAT, J. ROMAINS, B. TERNOVETZ, Paris, April 1931. — *Dessins de Matisse*, special issue of *Cahiers d'Art*, No. 3-5, Paris 1936. — Special number of *Le Point*, articles by H. MATISSE, R. HUYGHE, J. PUY, G. BESSON, R. COGNIAT, Lanzac, July 1939. — *De la couleur*, special Matisse issue of *Verve*, No. 13, essays by E. TÉRIADE and A. ROUVEYRE, Paris, November 1945. — *Art Présent*, No. 2, 1947, devoted in part to Matisse, under the direction of G. DIEHL, texts by H. MATISSE, F. ELGAR, E. PIGNON, J. CASSOU, G. POULAIN. — *Les miroirs profonds*, illustrated by MATISSE, texts by ARAGON, AUBRAY, BATISTINI, BLANCHARD, BREST, CAILLOIS, CHAR, DECAUNES, DERMENGHEM, DESRIVES, ELUARD, HUGNET, JAGUER, KOBER, LACOTE, LELY, LESCURE, MARCHAND, RIGAUD, DE SOLIER, SPYRIDAKI, TARDOS, Maeght, Paris 1947. — *La Chapelle de Vence*, special issue of *L'Art Sacré*, No. 11-12, July-August 1951, text by Father COUTURIER. — *Henri Matisse*, in *Yomiuri*, Tokyo 1951. — *Art News*, 1952 Annual, No. 21, essays on Matisse by G. SALLES and E. TÉRIADE, November 1951. — *Biennale di Venezia*, No. 26, 1955. — *Verve*, No. 35-36, texts by P. REVERDY and G. DUTHUIT, Paris 1958.

Chief Magazine Articles

L. VAUXCELLES, *Gil Blas*, October 14, 1904, and October 5, 1906. — A. GIDE, *Promenade au Salon d'Automne*, *Gazette des Beaux-Arts*, December 1905. — G. APOLLINAIRE, *La Phalange*, December 18, 1907. — B. BERENSON,

Letter to the Editor, *Nation*, November 12, 1908. — ESTIENNE, *Les Nouvelles*, April 12, 1909. — H. MERCEREAU, *Zolotoye Runo* (Golden Fleece), Moscow 1909. — G. STEIN, *Henri Matisse*, *Camera Work*, New York, August 1912; reprinted in *Twice a Year*, Fall-Winter 1946-1947. — M. SEMBAT, *Les Cahiers d'Aujourd'hui*, April 1913. — G. APOLLINAIRE, *L'Intransigeant*, April 28, 1913. — F. TUGENDHOLD, *The French Collection of S.I. Schukin*, *Apollo*, Nos. 1-2, 1914. — W. PACH, *Why Matisse?*, *Century Magazine*, February 6, 1915. — M. and A. LEBLOND, *La Vie*, January 1918. — R. SCHWOB, *L'Amour de l'Art*, October 1920. — H. PURRMANN, *Über Matisse*, *Genius*, 1920. — L. SWANE, *Matisse i Tetzen Lunds Samling*, *Tilskueren*, September 16, 1922. — L. WERTH, *Les Cahiers d'Aujourd'hui*, No. 8, 1922. — F. FELS, *Propos d'artiste*, *H. Matisse*, *Les Nouvelles Littéraires*, January 5, 1924. — J. GUENNE, *Entretiens avec Henri Matisse*, *L'Art Vivant*, September 15, 1925. — F. WATSON, *The Arts*, January 1927. — A. WARNOD, *Les Arts à Paris*, July 1927. — M. TOZZI, *Rouault e Matisse*, *Le Arti Plastiche*, Milan, November 16, 1927. — E. TÉRIADE, *L'Intransigeant*, January 14, 1929. — S. RATEL, *Visite au Musée de Grenoble*, *L'Art Vivant*, 1929. — F. NEUGASS, *Die Kunst*, Munich, October 1929, and *Cahiers de Belgique*, March 1930. — A. LEVINSON, *Les soixante ans de Matisse*, *L'Art Vivant*, January 1, 1930, — R. HUYGHE, *Matisse et la couleur*, *Formes*, January 1930. — G. POULAIN, *Sculptures d'Henri Matisse*, *Formes*, November 1930. — W. GEORGE, *Le double aspect de Matisse*, *Formes*, June 1931. — P. COURTHION, *Rencontre avec Matisse*, *Les Nouvelles Littéraires*, June 27, 1931. — M. SCHAPIRO, *Matisse and Impressionism*, *Androcles*, February 1932. — C. ROGER-MARX, *L'œuvre gravé d'Henri Matisse*, *Arts et Métiers Graphiques*, No. 34, March 15, 1933. — L. GILLET, *La Danse d'Henri Matisse à Merion*, *Beaux-Arts*, May 26, 1933. — G. DUTHUIT, *The Vitality of H. Matisse*, *The Listener*, February 19, 1936. — E. TÉRIADE, *Minotaure*, No. 9, October 15, 1936. — H. DE MONTHERLANT, *En écoutant Matisse*, *L'Art et les Artistes*, July 1938. — P. FIERENS, *Emporium*, Bergamo, October 1938. — P. GUÉGUEN, *La sculpture d'un grand peintre*, *XXᵉ siècle*, December 1938. — L. GILLET, *Une visite à Henri Matisse*, *Candide*, February 24, 1943. — F. CARCO, *Souvenirs d'atelier*, *Die Kunst-Zeitung*, Zurich, August 1943. — L. DEGAND, *Les Lettres Françaises*, October 6, 1945. — G. DIEHL, *Conversations avec Henri Matisse*, *Les Arts et les Lettres*, Paris, April 19, 1946. — H. PURRMANN, *Werk*, June 1946. — F. KIMBALL, *Philadelphia Museum Bulletin*, March 1948. — G. DIEHL, *La Chapelle de Vence*, *Les Amis de l'Art*, October 1, 1948. — L. ARAGON, *Arts de France*, Nos. 23-24, 1949. — C. GREENBERG, *Nation*, March 5, 1949. — A. H. BARR, *Matisse, Picasso and the Crisis of 1907*, *Magazine of Art*, May 1951. — DANIEL-ROPS, *L'acte de foi de Matisse*, *Le Journal de Genève*, September 22, 1951. — A. LEJARD, *Les Amis de l'Art*, October 1951. — G. SALLES, *A Visit with Matisse*, *Art News*, November 1951. — E. TÉRIADE, *Matisse speaks*, *Art News*, November 1951. — A. E. HOLM, *Matisse's Kapell i Vence*, *Kunsten Idag*, No. 20, 1951. — M. LUZ, *XXᵉ Siècle*, January 1952. — J. T. SOBY, *Matisse Reconsidered*, *Saturday*

Review, January 5, 1952. — J. SCHNIER, *Matisse from a Psycho-analytical Point of View*, *College Art Journal*, XX, 1952-1953. — A. ROUVEYRE, *Matisse évoqué*, *Revue des Arts*, June 1956. — W. S. LIEBERMAN, *H. Matisse, Print*, August 1956. — G. DUTHUIT, *Material and Spiritual Worlds of H. Matisse*, *Art News*, October 1956. — R. ESCHOLIER, *D'où vient Matisse?*, *Prisme des Arts*, 4, 1956. — L. DEGAND, *Pour une revision des valeurs: Matisse, un génie?*, *Aujourd'hui*, II, 1956. — P. REVERDY, *Matisse dans la lumière et le bonheur*, *Verve*, No. 35-36, 1958. — G. DUTHUIT, *Le tailleur de lumière*, *Verve*, No. 35-36, 1958. — J. LEYMARIE, *Le jardin du Paradis*, *Les Lettres Françaises*, August 6, 1959. — J. LASSAIGNE, *La peinture sans limites*, *Les Lettres Françaises*, August 6, 1959.

Writings by Matisse

Notes d'un peintre, *La Grande Revue*, December 25, 1908; reprinted in full in G. DIEHL, *Matisse*, Tisné, Paris 1954 (complete English translation in A. H. BARR, *Matisse, His Art and his Public*, Museum of Modern Art, New York 1951). — *On Modernism and Tradition*, *The Studio*, May 9, 1935. *Divagations*, *Verve*, No. 1, December 1937. — *Notes d'un peintre sur son dessin*, *Le Point*, special issue, July 1939. — Statements in *Peintres d'Aujourd'hui*, *Comoedia-Charpentier*, June 1943. — Statements in *Les Problèmes de la peinture*, *Confluences*, Lyons 1945. — *Observations on Painting*, *Horizon*, London, March 7, 1946. — *Comment j'ai fait mes livres*, in *Anthologie du livre illustré*, Skira, Geneva 1946. — *Le chemin de la couleur*, *Art Présent*, 1947. — Texts from *Jazz*, Editions Verve, Paris 1947. — *L'exactitude n'est pas la vérité*, Catalogue of the A.P.I.A.W. Exhibition of his drawings, Liége 1948; English translation in Catalogue of the Matisse Retrospective, Philadelphia Museum of Art, 1948, and reprinted in A. H. BARR, *Matisse, His Art and his Public*, New York 1951. — Letter from Matisse to Henry Clifford, in Catalogue of the Matisse Retrospective, Philadelphia Museum of Art, 1948. — *Henri Matisse vous parle*, *Traits*, No. 8, March 1950. — *La Chapelle du Rosaire des Dominicaines de Vence*, preface by Henri Matisse, Vence 1951; English translation in A. H. BARR, *Matisse, His Art and his Public*, New York 1951. — Preface to the Matisse Exhibition, National Museum, Tokyo 1951. — *Lettre à Monseigneur Rémond, évêque de Nice*, *L'Art Sacré*, No. 11-12, 1951. — *Message à sa ville natale*, November 8, 1952, in Catalogue of the Musée Henri Matisse at Le Cateau-Cambrésis. — Preface for *Portraits par H. Matisse*, Sauret, Monte Carlo 1954.

Bibliographical Supplement

J. GUICHARD-MEILI, *Henri Matisse, son œuvre, son univers*, Paris 1967. — R. J. MOULIN, *Henri Matisse, Dessins*, Paris 1968. — J. RUSSELL, *The World of Matisse*, New York 1969. — L. ARAGON, *Henri Matisse, Roman*, Paris 1971. — M. DUTHUIT, *Catalogue raisonné de l'Œuvre de Matisse*, in preparation.

INDEX OF NAMES

LIST OF COLORPLATES

CONTENTS

THIS VOLUME OF THE SERIES "THE TASTE OF OUR TIME"
WAS PRODUCED BY THE TECHNICAL STAFF OF EDITIONS
D'ART ALBERT SKIRA. FINISHED THE TWENTY-EIGHTH DAY
OF MARCH NINETEEN HUNDRED AND SEVENTY-TWO.

TEXT AND ILLUSTRATIONS PRINTED BY

COLOR STUDIOS
AT IMPRIMERIES RÉUNIES S.A., LAUSANNE
AND PRESSES CENTRALES S.A., LAUSANNE

PLATES ENGRAVED BY GUEZELLE & RENOUARD, PARIS

PHOTOGRAPHS BY

*Hans Hinz, Basel (pages 3, 120, 123), Henry B. Beville, Washington (pages 31,
75, 88, 91, 97, 98, 99, 102, 106, 115), Louis Laniepce, Paris (pages 36, 113),
Frank Lerner, New York (pages 87, 90, 109), and by the photographic services
of the National Gallery, Oslo (page 58), the Statens Museum for Kunst, Copenhagen
(page 121), and the Musée Henri Matisse, Le Cateau (page 18).
Editions du Cercle d'Art, Paris, kindly supplied the photographic material for the
clichés reproduced on pages 26, 27, 35, 47, 51, 52, 53, 56, 57, 61, 62, 67, 68, 70,
79, 80, 80a, 80b, 82.*

PRINTED IN SWITZERLAND